The Oatmeal Stories

Robert R. Stevens

Copyright © 2014 Robert R. Stevens
Printed by CreateSpace, an Amazon Company
CreateSpace, Charleston, SC
Available on Kindle and other devices.

Cover photo: Russell and Dorathy Stevens with
(left to right) Robert, Thomas, and Wesley.

ISBN: 1499170327
ISBN-13: 978-1499170320

Introduction

My dad, Robert Russell Stevens, is the oldest of the five children in his family and for that reason he bore the burden of helping his father not only with chores, but whatever else was necessary for their survival.

It was a difficult time during the 1940's, and life was a constant struggle for his family. He often told us how he went without shoes in the summer, sat alone during school lunch so no one would notice that he had nothing to eat, and slept in the cold attic where snow would drift in under the eaves and onto his back. I referred to these as "the oatmeal stories," because he also frequently told us about the times they ate nothing but oatmeal for days. I didn't appreciate these tales. I supposed they were being told for the purpose of making us grateful for what we had. When I set out to write a children's book about growing up in Maine during simpler times and asked my dad to relate some of his experiences, he began sending stories to me each day via email. Suddenly I was opening my inbox with anticipation, excited to read each new account of his childhood. I was amazed and saddened by what I read. These were not suitable for a children's book; nevertheless, I thought they should be told. These are the oatmeal stories.

Catherine A Serrao

Robert's mother, Dorathy, is standing by the well.
The shed, chicken house, and barn are in the
background. The wagon is loaded with boxes for
smelts. 1949

The old homestead

I don't remember moving back from Massachusetts to Surry, but I do remember the place we lived in was originally up on the old homestead that belonged to my grandmother. It was a one-room camp that my Uncle Irving built. We put it on skids, and two trucks hooked together dragged it down the road to the 100-acre lot my father bought for 400 dollars. His diary from that time simply stated, "The Will Thorn place mine now." We lived in that one room for a long time before my father built on. Funny what you remember sometimes. When the shack was still at Nanny's up on the hill, the water had to be lugged from somewhere (there was no well on that site) and my mother would just throw the dirty dishwater right out the window onto the ground. It was always muddy in that spot and my brother Tommy would play there. My mother kept saying to him, "Keep the hell out of there or I will dump the dish water on you!" Anyway, without thinking, my mother dumped the dishwater out the window right on Tommy. He always remembered that and thought she did it on purpose.

There was never any indoor plumbing or running water. My father told me once that if I dug a trench from the well to the house, he would put a hand pump in and make it easier to have water. I must have been only thirteen or fourteen. I dug a trench like he wanted with a pickaxe and shovel across the driveway to the house. The digging was as hard as you might imagine with the driveway packed down from years of travel. All summer long the trench stayed open, with us all jumping over it and driving as close as possible. Finally, in the fall, it was filled back in and there was no pump at the sink until years later. My father did not really want it. Did not want an inside bathroom either, because, as he said, "The old lady will use more water and the well won't take it."

If we used too much water, someone had to go to the well and get more. It was just an old hand-dug affair, about ten or twelve feet deep. At any time it could have been dug deeper with a back hoe tractor. In the winter the well top would be ice-covered. Sometimes there was not even a proper cover at all, so a person could easily slip and fall into the well. Only about

1

twelve feet deep, but head first, and that would be the end of you.

We had a small wood stove that would go out soon after we went to bed, and that was usually quite early. Remember, we had no radio or television in the early years. There was not even electricity on our road, so we only had kerosene lights. We were almost always out of oil for the lamps. The wicks would not reach the oil, so we would put water in the lamps so the oil would rise to the top and reach the wicks. This would only work for a while, and then the fire would just burn the wicks and smoke.

There were just bare studs in the house and no insulation. Nobody used it then. Tommy and I slept on a mattress in the attic, really just a crawl space, and our bedding consisted of the old coats men used to wear, long and usually wool. Once you got them on top of you, you could not move around a lot because they would fall off. You didn't want to leave your arms out because it would get very cold in that house. There was a trap door above the heating stove, about two by two feet. We would climb up the ladder that was nailed to the wall and that was where we slept. Probably was a hazard. Any fire and we would have had trouble. The roof above our head was so low that we could not stand up in the center, and when in bed, we could not sit up because the roofing nails came through and stuck down and you could hit your head on them. To get dressed, you would have to kick your pants on and then get on your knees to buckle up. Then you would go down the hole in the ceiling, and down the wall. When the stove was not running, I could step on it and get down. When the stove was running, it got very hot, and I would have to swing over out of the way and step down on loosely piled wood.

Our house was small, and it was either very hot or very cold. Water did freeze in our water pail on cold nights. To make extra room in the summer, we took the heating stove outdoor, just behind the fence. We had sort of a picket fence, and a lot of stuff went behind that. The kitchen ceiling was just boards with cracks in them. We could lie on our mattresses and look down into the kitchen, and there was nothing to stop the heat from coming up. The only ventilation we had was a small window that was low, maybe seven or eight inches off the floor, and we could lay our heads on the window sill and get some relief.

From that window in the attic, we watched the great fire on Mount Desert Island. I was seven years old. It was a big thing. Everyone talked about it and everyone knew someone that worked on that fire. From my view, I could see quite well, especially when the fire reached the higher elevations of the island. It was a great loss. A lot of the people who came regularly every summer and contributed to the economy never came back. It completely changed the island community.

By the time school got out in the spring, it was just like an oven in that attic. When Tommy and I had a chance to get out of there, we did. Sometimes we slept in the small barn until way after school started in the fall. You know something? That barn. When you see the picture of my mother standing by the well, you see it was a pretty small barn, yet at the time it seemed big to me. It was just a tar paper shack to keep the horse in, with a little room for some hay. Nothing more than a hovel, when you think about it. The hay loft was only about eight by eight feet square, but big enough to sleep in.

One year we had an old canvas tent that we set up in the field, and the night of the last day of school we stayed in that tent. It rained all night and we got wet, but the worst part was I woke up very sick. I had no idea what it was, but I was all swollen under my chin. It was the mumps. And getting cold and wet seemed to make it a lot worse. I had to stay in the house and it was a week before I could get back to my "summer home."

When we did get electricity, about the time I was ten years old, it was only a couple of plugs and a couple of pull chain lights, nothing fancy. We had nothing to run anyway, no toaster or anything. It was during this same time when I saw my first TV program, if you can call it that. I would walk three miles to where my father got his hair cut and ride back with him. See, the haircut was timed to a Gillette prize fight. The TV was all snowy and you could barely see anything, but I was not allowed to get there early enough to see the whole fight anyway, only in time to ride back with my father.

Dorathy, on left, with Aunt Mary, Irving's wife, holding Connie. In the foreground are Walter, Wesley, Tommy, and Sandra. The tar paper barn in the background is where Robert slept in the summer. c. 1949

The way we lived

When we were small, just before we went down to the bus, my mother would grab anything to wash our faces and most often it was the dish rag. I remember it always had a sour smell. With a limited water supply, I suppose my mother never washed the dish rags at all. The towel we would wipe up on hung just to the right of the stove on a nail and would be there for weeks. Everyone wiped up on it. It was the only thing to use. We didn't think anything about it. If we needed to wipe the baby's face, we would just spit on a piece of paper or a rag. Messy diapers would sit in a pail for a long time. There was no toilet to rinse them in. It sure made the house smell sweet. Do you remember cloth diapers? No, probably not.

A pail of water sat to the left of the kitchen sink and there was a dipper with the end of the handle bent over so the dipper would not slide into the bucket. Everybody drank from that dipper, and it never got washed. Neither would the pail. The sink itself drained out the wall of the kitchen and onto the ground. We washed up at that same sink.

When we grew up, you would stand at the sink with a wash basin and wash up as far as possible, and down as far as possible. Possible did not get washed as regular as it should be. Did I tell you about when we had baths? This was always on a Sunday night, but rarely on a regular basis. We would have to lug in enough water to fill the galvanized metal wash tub. Starting with the smallest, my brother Walter, we would take turns until we were done. We would have to add hot water to keep it warm, but never changed it. I would, of course, be last. The whole of us kids got impetigo once. It was a childhood disease that would generally go through the whole school. It was a skin problem that would give you scabs all over your body. We had some sort of soap or something and we had to wash in that tub. The scabs had to be scrubbed off. It was a bloody mess.

My father would get piles, or hemorrhoids, and these were pretty bad. If you don't know what that is, it is when your bung hole comes outside. It would help to have grease, like bag balm, on your finger and push them back up. My father had a very bad time with them. We would watch him soak his butt in a basin of warm water. He was plagued with boils, too, and he would wear copper bracelets around his neck and wrist that were supposed to keep them away. I had piles and boils when I was younger, and there just wasn't anything like them. The boils were so painful and I sometimes got carbuncles too, which were even worse. I think maybe it had to do with not being able to keep clean enough.

We wore our clothes, it seems, forever, and our bed clothes would never be washed until summertime. Now I am just about a fanatic about washing up and consider myself a clean person. Funny that we made it through what today would not be acceptable and we did survive.

I remember one time waking up in the middle of the night and something was in my bed clothes and I could not figure out what it was. It was slimy and cold. I slept with it until daylight when I discovered that the cat had had kittens that were stillborn. I cleaned up the mess the best I could. Having the bed clothes washed or cleaned was out of the question.

The cat never had a name and lived for 13 or 14 years. We just called her Mother Cat. She mostly slept in my bed. Not a bed, really, just a mattress on the floor. I suppose she had some peace there. I could always hear her coming. She had to climb up the living room wall to get up through the trap door where I slept. She only ate a little canned milk in a cup saucer – never had any special food that I can think of. Mostly she hunted for her food. One time Mother Cat was on the cupboard and jumped onto my father's back. She got thrown clear across the room.

We had to do away with our own pets, drown our own kittens. I did that a lot. My sister Sandra had to do the same thing. If the kittens were not feeding on the mother or there were too many that needed food, Sandra had to put them in a sack along with a rock and leave them on the beach at low tide. I didn't have to shoot any dog of ours, though. That was something my father would do. I was told to shoot any dog that came into our yard, and one time I shot two dogs in less than a minute. My father was pleased, at least. It was rare for us to have a dog very long. If it barked unnecessarily, it would be shot on the spot. To this day, I have never gotten attached to any animal.

If a dog of ours ever bit one of us kids, he would have been shot within that day, but we did have a goose that terrorized us. A goose bite will not usually bring blood, but they can take a pretty good bite that really hurts, and every time we would go outside he would never fail to attack us. I was the oldest, about eight or nine, and I could get to him after the first bite (sometimes even before he bit) and grab him by the neck. He would try to attack again and he was heavy, but I could fling him around and get out of his way. All our animals were allowed to roam around the yard, and sometimes in the house, with the exception of that goose. I don't know what happened to him but he sure was ugly and mean. Looking back, I think my father probably shot him. He was just like the ducks we had once. They were supposed to have some purpose, but all I could see they did was poop everywhere and become a nuisance.

The men in our family never went any farther than the doorstep to pee, that step being no more than four by four feet square. My mother would squat just around the fence by the house, no more than 10 or 15 feet away. As far as I know that ground would have been covered with at least urine, adding to the smells next to our kitchen door, and during the winter months we never went far from the house to do our other business. It was embarrassing to see the blood in the snow where my mother went and the sanitary napkins just everywhere it seemed.

My mother did not ever wash the outside of any cooking pans – never did up until the day she died. She only washed the inside. If you wanted to heat something up quickly you would take the covers off the top of the wood stove and set the pan right over the fire, so obviously they would get quite dirty. With only cold water most of the time, nothing got cleaned like it should have. Even when we killed and cleaned our chickens, we hardly ever washed properly.

When I think about it, we almost never had any way to keep things cold. An ice man would come in the summer and if we had some money we bought a small piece of ice from him. We had no refrigeration, so my father nailed a box on the side of the house with a screen nailed to it to keep the bugs out. The perishables, like margarine, would go in there, but in the summer it would melt. Canned milk or butter stayed on the kitchen table and the milk would dry up and fill the holes on the top of the can. We would clear them out with a fork or knife to use it. I can't remember anything spoiling or going bad, though I am sure a lot of stuff did. Now we worry about leaving something out of the refrigerator for any length of time, but back then if we had chicken sandwiched in mayonnaise, it did not matter how hot it got sitting out. It always got eaten. Huh! It makes you wonder.

There was no cellar, and no place to store canned things, so after the summer people would leave in the fall, we would use their cellars. We used one summer house that was about two miles down the road and when my mother needed something we would take a sled and walk down, open the place up, and get what we needed. Anything we had at our house would have frozen up solid during those cold nights without heat. As I got older my parents would holler to me to wake up and build a fire. Once I got the fire going, I would go back to bed until the house warmed up a bit.

My mother would get some fresh milk left down with the mail sometimes. At that time, mail men would bring things from the store in Surry. This usually went on the tab or you paid the mailman for it. (Also, that was how you ordered from the Sears Roebuck. Get a mail order from the postman one day and mail out the order the next.) This was before they started doing anything like pasteurizing and homogenizing. On freezing days the cream would come right out of the top of the glass milk bottle several inches. The bottles were tapered so they would not break when frozen. For us kids, milk was the canned concentrated Carnation brand. We put about one third milk in a glass, than added water from the water pail. After WWII, we had powdered milk that was developed for the servicemen. It didn't amount to much and did not mix well.

What we had for butter was not really butter. In the middle to late 1940's, it came in a plastic bag. It was the color of lard and about the same consistency. Right in the center of the bag was a spot of yellow substance that you would break and knead the bag so it all became the same color. It did not taste any better than you would expect. I can remember ration cards that would allow us to get gas. That was another thing during the war.

Dorathy Mack Stevens with Walter, Sandra, & Wesley, in front of the original one-room house. Steps were granite blocks from the old cellar, about 20 feet away. 1949

The oatmeal stuck out in my mind

I remember one time when there was hardly anything left to eat, my father and I broke into this barn up the road and stole some beans that had been left on the barn floor. They had been there for many years. We threshed them out and they were like little rocks, they were so hard. My mother could not bake them, so she boiled them. They had little things like worms that came out when they split. I said to my father, "They look like worms." He said, "They are, but don't say anything. The other kids won't eat them."

My mother would send me up to the store, three miles, to get something on credit and I would have to walk back home the three miles without anything. Most of the time our credit was dried up and they would not let me have anything.

They did give us some tripe one time. It was probably bad already. Tripe is the lining of a cow's stomach. What we had was pickled and my mother fried it in bacon fat. That was bad enough, but she described in detail what it was (one of her "off" moments, I guess.) Anyway, it did not taste very good and I would gag when I tried to eat it. She would force me. I would go outdoors and throw up, come back and eat more, and go back outdoors again. That was how I had to eat that crap and I will never eat tripe again. They gave us some chocolate candy bars once. Turns out they had worms in them. We got them free and we ate them, just not the worms. The worms stayed in the peanuts. The chocolate was good.

There was no welfare. We never got anything. My father would not have stood for that. We would eat rolled oats for days at times, three meals a day. The oatmeal was boiled up in the morning, though my mother never got the knack of doing it the same way twice, so it could be dry one morning, gooey the next. At noon time we would fry what was left over from breakfast with old bacon fat we got from Danny Sexton who lived next door. Sometimes we would spread molasses or jelly or something like that on it to make it more palatable. We had it a lot, but I never did know where it came from. As I've mentioned, most of the time we did not have any credit at the store, yet we always seemed to have the oatmeal.

Recently I was talking with my sister Sandy about old times, and she said, "Thank God for the mail lady leaving the oatmeal and flour at the mailbox." It was Esther Carter who delivered the mail. Esther was married to Forest who owned the Surry store and tagged the deer and sold them for my father for a price. She would know when my father was laid up, sick, or out of work. She was a bit of a gossip and anyone coming into the store would know anything she might know and she would find out anything they might know. Along with the mail, she would drop off rolled oats and bags of flour. Guess that is why the oatmeal stuck out in my mind. It saved our hides I am sure. There was not a lot to eat sometimes, and I don't remember any time complaining about it, no matter how it was cooked.

Many times we would eat smelts from the bay where my father would fish in the winter. We would eat those fish until we got a check from the Boston fish market for the fish he caught and sold. Then we could buy some food from the store, but we would not have much money left after catching up on our bill.

When I was old enough to babysit, my mother and father left me with my siblings. Probably they were only going to the Surry store, but I began looking for something that might be good to eat. I found some rind of bacon, like you would put into beans to cook. Actually there was nothing left. It should have been thrown away. I cut it into pieces and was frying it up to eat when they came home. I got slapped around a lot for that and it got dumped out, so I didn't even get to taste it.

One of my favorite foods growing up (that I still like) is hot pork scraps and molasses. This is how you fix it: First cut up the pork fat in very small pieces and fry it up in a pan so you end up with a lot of small scraps of pork and a lot of fat. Pour some of that hot fat in a dish and add some of the scraps, then pour molasses into the middle of it. Add a pan of hot biscuits and you've got yourself a meal! I still eat molasses with a couple of slices of bread for dessert once in a while. You've seen me do that.

There is something that happened to me once that scared me quite bad. We had eaten pickled beets one night, and I drank the juice left over in the jar. The next day, I went out back to pee and it was blood red. Man, I was scared. I did not have anyone to talk to about it, and all that day every time I went to do my business, number 1 or number 2, it was blood red. I was old enough to think my days were numbered. It cleared up after a day, but I kept thinking it was going to come back on me. It was a long time later when I figured out what I had done. Funny what you remember about things like that.

One thing that me and my father shared was pickled pig's feet and a stick of kielbasa (polish sausage). It was one thing he would buy when he had money and I don't think any of the other kids liked them. Boy, it sure was a treat for me. I still like polish sausage but I can leave the pig's feet alone.

I remember my father coming home and we would get any of his leftover lunch for the day. It was just a little coffee in a jar and maybe a piece of sandwich, but I would get it as soon as he pulled into the yard.

First family reunion – Robert's cousins.
George, Robert, Thomas, Sandra,
Walter, Steven, Nancy, Albert (hiding,)
Cindy, and Wesley, at Surry Bay, 1955

We played hard

We kids threw everything at each other, and one way we would while away our time was with apple fights. We would whittle out a short stick making it sharp on one end and then place the apple on the tip. We could throw a long way with a great deal of accuracy, and we would get behind things for protection, but it did not always stop us from getting hurt.

My cousin Jimmy and his brothers were fighting against me and Tommy one time, and we were hiding out behind a couple of wood piles. I threw an apple and hit Jimmy in the eye. Man, it must have hurt. It was all we could do to talk him out of going to our parents to tell.

Well, things were going along quite well, and we got back into flinging apples again. I threw another apple and it hit Jimmy in the other eye. There was no hope for me then. I got a whipping right there and then, in front of everyone. Had it coming though. How can that happen twice in a row?!

We played hard. It was common for us to have rock fights. You couldn't help getting hit. Probably the most dangerous thing was shooting at each other with BB guns. You could aim those things and even when you got hit in the back of the head, it sure hurt! Amazing that I still have two eyes!

We kids often played with slingshots. Do you know, if you take a leather tongue out of an old shoe and tie a couple of long rawhide strings with a loop on one end, you have a slingshot. We would put a rock in the center and swing it around a few times and let go of one of the strings. That rock could be sent with accuracy for hundreds of feet. It was really easy to make. Think of the pictures you have seen of Goliath in the Bible being killed by a slingshot. Same thing, but another thing that kids probably should not play with. We did make bows and arrows that were not very accurate, but they were fun. Guns were always leaning in one corner of the house and there were always sharp knives, but no one seemed to worry about us getting hurt. We would whittle whistles, mostly out of alder wood, and they worked quite well. We would whistle on grass stems. We always found something to do. Pretty much, if we stayed outside, we could do about anything.

When the electricity was hooked up, Tommy and I would stick our fingers in the outside light socket and see who could do it the longest. There was never any bulb in there anyway. It never occurred to us that we could die. We did that a lot. Think about it now and it sounds kinda dumb. Make ya tough? Maybe.

On Easter Sunday, there was a dare to get into the Surry Bay with the ice still on the shore and jump in. I guess I would do anything on a dare. It was thought you would be tough if you could let someone stand on your stomach – just lay on your back on the floor and let someone stand right on your stomach. I did it, and it sure impressed the whole class. Actually, your stomach muscles have to be good and strong. Think about it. If I did it now, it would put me in the hospital, maybe the funeral home.

We had some good times

We never had sleds, so sliding was done on cardboard or something slippery. Before there was plastic, we had barrel staves, the boards of the side of an old wooden barrel. We drilled holes through them, and then tied them to our feet with strings to make skis. Not good, but slippery. We could wax them with paraffin wax like the kind we would put on the top of jars of jelly to keep the mold out.

Some people down the road came by one day and noticed what we were doing and asked us if we had sleds. "Nope," we said. A couple of days later they brought us a couple of *Cape Racers*, metal runner sleds. Can you imagine how we liked that?

The same couple asked my parents if they could take Tommy and me to the circus in Bangor one summer. My parents agreed, and a few days later they came back and told us we did not have to wear shoes to the circus if we did not want to. They probably knew we did not have any. Our footwear was pretty worn out about the time school was over each spring.

We actually had one of those wagon wheel hoops that you have seen in old pictures that kids would run alongside with a stick and keep it rolling. We never seemed to get tired of running, and I could run for a long time.

There were two big rocks that we played on. One was just out into the woods probably a few hundred feet, and we would always show it off to any one of my cousins or anyone else that might visit us. It was probably only ten feet high, but we were barely three or four feet, and with no easy climbing sides, it was a challenge for us. You have to remember that we did not have many things we could show off.

The other big rock was in the water where we went swimming. When the tide was high, we could see two rocks just barely showing, so we knew where to find them. It was quite a few years before I could get to the first rock. I was small enough so I could not stand up without being under water. It was really something if you could swim long enough to get to the second rock. This may not seem like a big deal

17

now, but it was a big deal then. It was well into my high school years before I swam in fresh water. I could always open my eyes under the salt water, but could not ever do it in fresh water without discomfort.

Actually, we had some good times on the shore across from our house. The beach was pretty nice and there was hardly anyone ever coming to the cottages down on the shorefront. When they did arrive, they would only stay for a week or so.

We had a small wooden boat with a flat bottom which leaked pretty badly. We kids were allowed to row out into the bay, and especially at mackerel time, we might catch something. If we caught sculpins, they had spines that would get into our feet and hands. We had trouble just getting them off the hook because we could not hold them and they would not die in the bottom of the boat because there was so much water. We would have to row back to the shore and leave them on the beach.

We kids would play with just about anything. We were picking up snails that gathered on the rocks and we had about half a pail full of them when someone from England who was renting a summer cottage offered us a dollar and asked if we could get more. Tommy and I took the dollar and said, "Yes, we can get more." While they were watching, we went right down like fools and got another pail full in a few minutes. That was our last dollar. They picked them up themselves from then on. They boiled them and picked them out with a toothpick. Nasty, I thought.

There was a little island called Goose Rock, just off the very end of Newberry Neck which could only be accessed at low tide. My father dropped me and Tommy off just when the tide was right and picked us up the next day. There was a gate lock on the access road but of course that was no problem for my father. We woke up the next morning to see a herring boat just off shore. The island was very small and the fishermen were surprised to see two small boys hollering to them from that little rock of an island.

We heard that the upchucking of a whale (the ambergris) was used for perfume. I would walk the beaches for hours looking for it. We were told that it was very expensive and would bring a lot of money if found. Being ignorant, we never realized that whales would not be in that area, and even what it might look like if we found some, but it sure kept my interest for several years.

That was the most fun after a long winter – walking around the shore and seeing what had drifted up. It was peaceful. Staying in the house was not pleasant and my mother kicked us out in any kind of weather anyway, so we were outside a lot. I guess it did not hurt me.

One spring, we discovered a log that had been hollowed out by someone, like the dugouts that you see on TV that native Indians would dig out or burn out to use for a boat. It had washed up on our beach and it was so heavy it took us kids a long time to get it down to the beach far enough to have it float. I mean weeks! Eventually we lost interest in it. It was not very seaworthy.

They did catch flies

Boy, I sure can remember that the house was always full of flies and bugs, and we always had hens, roosters, and sometimes ducks around the house. There was bird poop everywhere. As I've mentioned before, the house was hot in the summer and I can't remember if we had screens or not, but the doors were always open to let what breeze there was blow in. My father had a couple of ideas for both bugs and hens. He would cut strips in a newspaper page almost to the top of the page and then he would tack the page above the door. He thought the blowing or waving of the strips would scare off the flies. If that didn't work, he had those nasty, sticky, poison strips that would hang from the ceiling. The problem was, they were hardly ever taken down and they hung down over the table and would hit you in the head. They did catch the flies though.

For the hens, he built a screen door of chicken wire with its thin, one-inch circles. It kept the chickens out when the door was closed, but they were always getting into the house and had to be shooed out. We went barefoot all summer and because of the hens we were always stepping in poop. Also, we would cut our feet on the lids of tin cans or old nails lying about. We got used to walking on our toes or heels. There were no band aids. A rag with an old piece of salt pork was the only thing we put on it. It was supposed to suck out the poison, I guess.

When the chimney needed cleaning, my father would open the "clean out" (small door at the base of the chimney) and start a fire with rags soaked with kerosene and let her burn. Flames would come out the top of the chimney for several feet! He tried to do it when there was not any traffic on the Neck because people would always stop and tell him, "You've got flames coming out of the chimney!" My father would tell them, "Hell, yeah, I know! It will go out sometime."

I don't know why the house did not burn down with my father's chimney trick and my mother frying clams or shrimp and the fat rolling right over the pan she was cooking in and onto the old gas range she cooked on. When I was young, it was only a wood cook stove. The gas stove was long after I moved out. It was easier to cook on in the summer heat.

My mother's ringer washing machine always stayed outdoors, winter and summer. We would just bring it in when she washed. My mother also had a sewing machine that she would use on the door step. It was a treadle machine, which meant working it with your feet. It made a vibration that you would not think much about, but apparently the night crawlers thought it was a rain storm and they would come out of the ground. Huge, long things would come over the door step and into the area of the sewing machine. Not just a few; a lot of them. It was a weird thing to happen and I never forgot it.

Robert's mother, Dorathy, in the kitchen. Robert slept just above this, in the little attic.

It was quite a hole

All the time I grew up and lived at home, the old camp we lived in sat just behind an old cellar hole, about 25 feet away. An old house sat there at one time and was either torn down or burned. It was quite a hole, probably six feet deep at least and about 18 by 20 feet square. My father planned to have it bulldozed and filled in, but he never had money to do it, so it stayed open for many years 'til long after I was gone from the house. He would throw garbage in it and anything he figured would be covered over some day. It was a dangerous spot for young kids growing up. It was a great place for snakes, and we had a lot of snakes. I mean a lot of them – big ones. They were always around where we would be playing.

One day I saw a really big one, more than two feet, so I grabbed the axe that was always around. I got alongside the snake and cut it in half. She was full of snakes, more than a dozen, all very much alive. The problem was that when I cut it in half, it sprayed blood and fluid all over my face and body. Now, remember, I had no place to wash up, no bathroom, only a well that by that time of year was probably dry. We had no water. The only thing to do was run as fast as I could go across the road and plunge into the bay. Man, snakes never impressed me too much. God must have a reason for them. I don't.

The outhouse

I almost forgot about the outhouse. That was an ordeal sometimes because in the winter it was so cold. I will tell you more about the slop jar later. That was mostly for my mother, though during the night I am sure my father used it too. It was always full and so nasty, and as I got older it was my problem to empty it, not in the outhouse, just outdoor somewhere behind the house or closer in the winter when the snow was deep. Nobody cared as long as it wasn't in the house. It never was rinsed out. Who wanted to lug water from our well for that? So I guess it stunk when I put it back in their bedroom, but the outhouse was never pleasant. I think about the stories that are written by outhouse enthusiasts, how lovely, how you can think things over, how you looked at the catalog and ordered when you got back into the house. Bull!

Our outhouse was almost always full enough to touch your bottom when you sat down, and I remember having to dig it out at least once. (Being oldest has its drawbacks.) You would take a stick and push it down or knock the top off to one side. Because nobody wanted to clean it out on a regular basis, you would have to stand up on the seat and squat down to do your business. In summer you just used paper or leaves if there were any and went into the woods and did what you had to do. It sounds untrue, but it really is true. There was a Sears catalog or magazine, just like the stories you have heard. We rarely had a roll of toilet paper. Sometimes my mother kept a roll for her in the house, but we kids didn't get to use it. Being a mother in our house had some perks also, I guess.

I hated the whippings

Boy, I hated the whippings I would get. I am sure that I had it coming a lot of the time, but I think my mother really enjoyed doing it. I would always have to go into the woods and get my own switch. It had to be just right. If it broke on us, I would have to go get another and it had to be limber enough to hurt, and believe me, she would not stop sometimes. It always left welts and hurt for hours and sometimes days because it did not matter to her where she hit me, though most of the time it was the butt area.

I remember one time I had gotten the switch and she was hitting me and I grabbed the switch and took it away from her. I had to run. I did not think I would be able to live there anymore. I ran into the woods and kept thinking of where I could go. I knew the way through the woods to the back shore and how to get to a road, but did not know what I would do after that. Anyway, my father had just come home and my mother told him what happened and where I had run to. He came into the woods and hollered to me. After he hollered a few times, I answered him and then ran like hell again, but every time he hollered I would answer, so eventually he caught up with me and gave me a hug. That was the only time I ever remember him doing that. We had a long walk back to the house and my mother was there with her own switch she had gotten and was going to start again. My father told her no, and I did not get another whipping that time. When we got back, my Uncle Red had just come into the driveway and he said, "Hell, if I had a dollar for every time I ran away from home, I would be rich." I was embarrassed enough. I did not need that.

My mother really did like to hit me, I think. If it was in the house, I might be hit with anything: a wash cloth or a dish rag would hurt a lot. In the face was one thing, but it would wrap around and hurt all over. She would say, "I will give you Old Lady Palm and her five daughters," or "I will slap you hard enough to make your nose bleed buttermilk." She was always using her hand. I remember one time being hit so hard that my ears rang for a long time. I was old enough to know that I could go deaf, so I would put my hand over one ear and then the other to see if I could tell the difference in my hearing.

I am not sure just how old I was, but it is a hard thing to forget. I don't know what prompted it, but it must have been something I said or did. She hollered at me, telling me to say I was sorry, but before I could say anything, she grabbed me by the hair and pulled my head back over the kitchen chair. She had a kitchen knife at my throat and I could feel the blade. I was old enough to know it would not take much to cut it with my head back so far. I would have said anything, but as hard as I wanted to, I could not talk. You can't talk with your head pulled back like that. Try it sometime. She kept screaming and I thought she really was going to do it. She was out of control. Of course, she did not do it, or I would not be here today, but I sure was scared.

Sandra, Wesley, Tommy, and Robert. c.1949

I was taught to steal

Someone got their car stuck once, went for help, and before they could get back to it, I had taken the starter, generator, wheels, tires, and so much stuff that it is still sitting where it was to this day. Sometimes if I asked my father where something came from, he would say, "Well, I took it from So and So. If I hadn't, someone might have stolen it!" If my father shot a deer at night and he could not find it in the dark, he would get us older kids up early before school and we would span out and walk through the woods until we found it.

I was taught to steal from a very young age, but apparently did not catch on as to *when* to steal and *when not* to steal. An example: One fall during hunting season, Gerald French and my mother's brother, Wesley, took my father and me to a hunting camp way up north of Route 9. I have no idea where it was but it seemed at the time we would never get there. We were in a car that does not exist today and most people have never heard of it – a *Kaiser*. It was a 1949 model. The *Frazer* was built that year also, and both were almost alike.

Anyway, we showed up at this camp and a couple of guys had already been there for a while, hunting. We stayed for a while, and during the visit I stole a couple of cans of tinned sardines from the shelf. On the way back, I proudly produced the cans of sardines and showed them to everybody. Well, my father gave me hell and said, "You never steal a man's food or a man's tools!" It makes sense, but that part of my lesson was never explained to me before. Go figure. Another thing he said, "If you get caught, don't lie, because they've already got you. It will only make things worse." He went to great lengths not to get caught at anything, and he did quite well at it.

I could have done anything

Moral values were almost non-existent in our family. I could have done anything and it would have been no big deal. We would do little things like spit and throw rocks at cars from the bushes or steal radiators and sell them to junk yards. My father would pick the locks on the summer houses and we would go in to see if there was anything we could use ourselves or sell for the cash.

He would get junk metal sometimes and sell it to the junk yards for cash. He didn't ever work regular jobs but kept busy cutting wood, fishing, and working for summer people during their season in Surry. He would cut hay and clear fields with a hand scythe and snath before they ever had motorized lawn mowers.

On the Cross Road beyond our house there was a church that was only used in the summer. We broke into that church, went down in the cellar, took the metal jacket off the heat furnace, then took a sledge hammer and broke up the cast iron. We threw the broken metal out of the cellar window and sold the junk. I was only about nine or ten years old. Early education, wouldn't you think?

Around that same time, I was using a sledge hammer to bust up some cast iron that my father "picked up" and brought home. I was in the field where we had a lot of stuff going to the junk yard. We had to break up anything that could be identified by anyone. For your information, cast iron breaks up like pottery. It doesn't bend; it just breaks off into pieces flying off in all directions. One piece hit me in the left eyebrow and was bad enough for me to bypass the "butterfly stitch" my father usually used. He took me to the hospital where I took four stitches. It would not look too good for a young boy to tell the doctor he was breaking up cast iron, would it now? So on the way to the hospital my father concocted a story that I fell down and cut myself. It was no problem for me. I always did what he asked.

When I was a little older, my father got jobs for many of the summer people – mowing, general repair, and just odd jobs. Well, anyway, he became a caretaker for a lot of them. About the time school started in the fall, they would go back home and would not be back until late in the spring. Some mowing would still have to be done, and any other jobs they wanted done after they left, my father would do and send them the bill. This gave him keys to most of the summer places - sort of letting the fox guard the chickens, huh? Those were the days when a lot of people burned wood and there was a problem of thieves breaking in during the winter and stealing stuff, especially stoves. You could always sell a used stove.

My father kept a running diary on their table to say what the weather was like, etc. when he was there so the summer people had quite a record of any work that was done during their absence. They loved it. It was a conversation piece for them all summer, showing their friends the book he left. Actually all the summer people liked him. They would invite him down to "settle up," and he gave them something to think and talk about. I am sure they did not know anybody like him.

One thing he would do is take the covers or maybe a door off their stove and hide the pieces. He would say, "Who in hell would be stupid enough to steal a stove without all the pieces?" He only got paid $50 to watch their places for the whole winter and sometimes he would even have to snow-shoe in to check the property. He took good care of them. It was a cheap deal for them and a little plus for him. He could often use the upstairs bedrooms to shoot deer from the window. The deer were baited and nobody would hear a shot from inside a house. It was a sure thing. We could use their garages for working on our cars and their cellars for storage of canned goods. Actually, when we needed an extra room for someone to stay, he would let someone sleep in one of their bedrooms. Not a lot, but it did happen.

What could I do?

I worked all fall and early spring mowing grass for a summer person. It was a push mower. There were no motors then. I had $18 coming and had my heart set on a second-hand bicycle. When my money came, we needed it for food.

I never did get my own bicycle until years later. We did have one that came from somewhere but it had no chain or pedals. This was before handlebar brakes. We could not stop until it came to a stop on its own or we could put our feet down and run with it and stop ourselves. We were constantly getting hurt, but we had a great time with it.

Boyd Smith and his wife were summer residents. He was a professor from Harvard. I don't think they had any children. They were straight-laced. When I got old enough, I started mowing their lawn. I was paid 50 cents an hour, so the money meant a lot to me. First, they had an old push mower which went along as hard as you can imagine. Eventually they got an electric mower which I used for a couple of years. To get it to work in the spring I had to go down cellar and flick a switch to get the electricity to work. Without knowing it, I flicked the wrong switch long enough to burn out one of the elements of their hot water heater.

When they got there in the summer, of course, their water did not heat up. When I came down with my father so they could settle up with us, they told us what had happened. I don't remember how much they owed me, but he told me that the money for the repairs had to be taken out of it. Boy, what a shock. I had less than $20 coming to me, and lost more than half for the repairs. I was thinking all winter what I might buy with that money. That was a hard lesson to swallow.

I worked for Henry Kane treading hay. The haying was always done by horse. First it was cut, a few days later it would be turned to dry, then it would have to be thrown up over the top of the wooden hay ricks onto a 4-wheeled wagon with tall sides to haul as much hay as possible in one load. To get as much as possible, it had to be trod down and moved around as someone on the ground forked it up. I got paid ten cents a day for that.

That must have been the going rate, because Percy and Bridget Kane paid me the same for a day's work hauling garbage out of their cellar that had been there all winter. Percy was a relative of Henry Kane, and Bridget came from England. It seemed Percy never worked and Bridgy, as everyone called her, was always saying, "Poor Perce, Poor Perce. He's not well." Seems like poor Percy Kane was sick. Even then, I thought he was just lazy. Never changed my mind about that.

By the age of 14, I was babysitting for the neighbors. One couple in Surry, Ralph and Loretta, would go out every Saturday night and get pretty drunk. They had a young woman, Henrietta, from Town Hill, who was always around them. She was an alcoholic and so were they. Loretta had two different-colored eyes. Henrietta was Ralph's girlfriend, but there was definitely something going on between Henrietta and Loretta. I would have to stay there all night because they would not get home until after 1:00 in the morning and they always came home drunk.

One time they were arguing and fighting and Ralph started hitting Loretta. She hollered to me for help. I got out of bed and ran into their bedroom. Ralph told me to shut up and get back to bed. So, what could I do? I went back to bed. At 14 years old, I could not have done much.

Robert's grandmother, Amanda Henry Stevens,
with Sandra Ellen Stevens. 1949

In between us boys

I remember when Sandy was young, perhaps four or five years old, her hair was very fine and blond, and you could see right through to her head. My father figured if he cut all her hair off, it would come back a little thicker, so it sort of got banged around between my mother and father for a while. It was a small battle, and as always, my father prevailed and her hair was all cut off. Well, she looked scalped, as you might think, and Sandy sure knew what was going on and was mad as hell. It did grow back thicker, though, so Daddy was right.

You know, she was right in between us boys, and I have thought many times about how she was treated. Us boys treated her like a boy, but let me tell you something. When she got to a certain point and could not take any more, she knew how to handle herself. I have seen her sling Walter and Wesley around more than once.

I remember the Reeds from Massachusetts. Harry and his wife were an older couple who only came up summers. They took a real liking to Sandy and when they were up, she spent quite a bit of time with them. That would have given her some outside contact beyond our family.

Sandra did *not* think the old days were much fun. There was a lot of work for her - cleaning, dishes, and washing clothes, without proper equipment to do it, and the boys were never made to help her. We only had the old cast iron sink with mostly cold water, so doing dishes would discourage just about anyone. My mother was not a good housekeeper, so she did not get much home training. She became an excellent seamstress, though my mother never taught her any of that.

Thomas Henry Stevens, sitting
on 1928 Chevy. 1944

Me and Tommy

My brother, Tommy, was a dreamer and would spend literally hours walking back and forth in a woods path behind the house pretending to be western characters like Lash LaRou, Tom Mix, Hopalong Cassidy, and others – fictional characters, comic book people. Remember, we did not have anything to listen to – no radio, no electricity. Even our cars did not ever have radios. Tommy would pace back and forth shooting, fist fighting, and doing a lot of action-talking. He would dress up with old clothes that would be in the old cars we always had around the house and field. We would both dress up, and we could fool Sandy, Wesley, and Walter into thinking we were actually one of those western characters. I really had some gullible siblings. Once we even talked Wesley into drinking kerosene and sucking eggs.

When Tommy and I were a little older, we sometimes got simple privileges that the younger kids did not. After they went to bed, we could share something that was left over from supper or a last piece of dessert. It could have been anything. Common practice was to have one cut it in half and the other had first choice. The one cutting it would measure and study it and finally divide it. Lots of times we would argue over who would get to cut it. We would draw straws for the honor. We did that a lot with decisions – drew straws.

Tommy was the favorite. It showed in a lot of ways. When we were going to get a whipping, Tommy would just run away far enough so that I would get mine first. My mother was about whipped out by the time she got to Tommy. He would lie down on the ground and kick his legs and she would slap at him a couple of times and laugh and quit.

If we wanted to do something and needed permission, it was always Tommy that had to ask. It was a definite *No*, if I asked. We both knew it and Tommy always would ask for whatever we wanted. It usually was something like leftovers from supper or something like that. Any favor we wanted, he had to ask. He was her favorite. I took care of what I had, but Tommy was very slack. For instance, we had to go outdoors, no matter what the weather, and one time we both had new mittens. Tommy lost one of his and my mother made me give mine to him.

I told you we had a horse and we would ride him some, just around the field. He was a work horse so was broad at the back. Our legs were stretched out, like riding on an old barn door – not comfortable at all. Anyway, we were taking turns riding him and when it was my turn, Tommy would not get off. I threw a small rock and hit the horse and up he went and Tommy went with him. When Tommy came back down, the horse was not there. He did get hurt, I guess, and my father gave me a licking, first and only time I remember.

My father did not think brothers should fight each other. Whenever we got into a scuffle and it looked like we were serious enough to do some damage to each other, he would really get upset and break it up, saying, "Brothers don't fight each other."

Tommy was a spunky guy. We were both fighters and we knew better than to come home and tell my father that we got beat up by someone at school. His theory was, "If the ---- gets up on one knee, that is too far." He was always showing us special holds and ways of fighting that apparently worked OK for him.

One day Tommy got into a row with someone, and we went off the high school grounds, several carloads of us, so we could watch them fight. They had been at it for quite a while when the other guy hit Tommy just right and broke his nose – just pushed it off sideways. Boy, that must have hurt! Anyway, it took a while to take care of it, but they went right back to fighting, and Tommy beat the crap out of him. It was just the way we grew up. Don't take anything from anybody. It took weeks for his nose to heal up.

I was fighting way up into the time I was married, in fact I got into a real whopper right in front of Cunningham's Grocery store in Ellsworth when you kids were small. I'll tell you about that some other time.

One night after Tommy and I went to bed in the loft in the barn, we were griping about the way we were treated. Unbeknownst to us, our mother had climbed up the ladder to the loft area and was listening to us. She finally heard enough and started in on us. Boy, was she furious! But things do happen once in a while that are sweet.

My father had just come back from hunting, well after dark, and saw her up on the ladder. He threw a piece of birch bark at her and hollered to scare her. Well, it worked. Man, oh man! Now she was mad, but guess who got it now? You got it! My father. Life was good.

One Rich Kid

A lot of people grow up with at least one rich kid around them. Mine was Vern. Vern grew up with his father and stepmother, and his stepmother's son was a lot older, so Vern got a lot of attention. His grandfather and grandmother had a store in Surry and they lavished everything on him, and I mean he had the latest of everything, including the latest motorized toys.

When I would occasionally go to his house, it seemed like a dream world. He had things that I did not know existed. Remember, our exposure to the outside world was the Sears Roebuck catalog, so it if was not in there, we had no way of knowing about it. Vern had a whole chest, like they would use years ago to travel abroad, full of the latest funny books. I could have read them for days, but it was old hat to him. He just wanted to move on to something else. He was nice, and though he would come down sometimes to play with me, he just could not understand how we lived so different from him. As I look back, it was no big deal for his grandparents to give him those things, and his father was a plumber just making a living like we do now. But back then I thought he was the richest kid alive.

I didn't see Vern for many years. He was a really nice guy and he became a teacher. After he retired, we met and talked several times and really seemed to hit it off. Vern was always very careful and followed rules and was safety conscious. Here's what surprised all of us who knew him: He went out on the ice with his snowmobile one morning and went through and drowned. He grew up on that little pond and had to know it better than anyone else.

We were scared to death

Tommy and I, age ten and eleven, walked from our house in Newberry Neck to the movie house on Main Street in Ellsworth. We each had a quarter and that was plenty. We saw a movie called "The Thing." It was one of the early thrillers of that time, released in 1951, about an alien that was frozen in the ice, then chopped out and put in a shed. The tender put an electric blanket on the block containing the alien, the ice melted, and the alien started eating people.

Well, it sure made a big impression on Tommy and me. We knew a lot about nothing, and we were a little superstitious too. We had to walk every step of the way home from the movie theater, 13 miles. (A walk of 13 miles home in the middle of the night was quite a thing as I think about it now. How many kids today would walk 13 miles for anything!?) We didn't get home until after midnight. Here's the problem: It was the first time in our lives that we saw the northern lights and they were the most spectacular I have ever seen. The sky flashed continuously and we were scared to death. It was the longest walk I have ever taken.

Dorathy and Russell Stevens,
Surry, Maine.

She would deny the things I have said

My mother was an avid reader and would read to us for hours when we were young. She would repeat poetry that she had learned in school – old Shakespeare stuff and other poems. She was good at it. If my father came home from work, or showed up suddenly, she stopped immediately. He probably never knew that she read to us. She would say to us kids, right in my father's presence, "Look at the old bastard. Your father's a stupid bastard. He barely knows how to read." She put him down in front of us, and he didn't say anything back to her. He only went as far as 4th grade, right there in Surry, but my mother went as far as her junior year in High School. Maybe that was the reason she made fun of him. She was living on the Surry Road and that is where she met my father. She was walking with someone he knew. She was 18 when they got married and he was 29.

She told us stories about her childhood and would get choked up talking about her brother's death. Some of her stories were funny, but most were about how abusive her father was when he came home drunk. Apparently he ruled the household and the whole family would cower in fear as he ranted and raved and broke things around the house.

My father drank a lot when I was young, and until I was about eight years old, he would go off with friends (drinking buddies) from Massachusetts. His buddies would come down to visit and my mother would never know when he might come home. She would let me get in her bed. I don't know why, but when she heard the car in the driveway, knowing my father was home, she would quickly get me out and in my own bed before he could get in the house. He never knew. We had some terrible winters then, with a lot of snow, and there were times that we had no wood for the fire. She and I would go out digging in the deep snow where we remembered there was some wood. One time we did break up some chairs to burn. My mother would cry when he didn't come home and again if he came home drunk.

We burned wood, and she was always letting the fire go out. She would get it burning very hot, not close the dampers, and the fire would burn itself out and have to be started again. She never got the hang of wood fires. It was like her driving. When we were older, she tried to take her test several times but she never had any concept of how to drive and she just would not listen to anyone. She never could get a license to drive.

My father was impatient with her and criticized her a lot. She was a lousy housekeeper, and he would always wipe his silverware on his shirt (which was probably dirty also) before he used it. He would call her filthy names, "Old Squaw," "Old Slut," or "Dumb B----." There were cigarette ashes on everything. In the bedroom, the slop jar was so full it could not be taken out and dumped without spilling some of it. When it was too full for her to move, it became my job. I hated it. I probably should explain about the slop jar. I think fancy people called it a commode, but nevertheless, it was something that you did your business in if you could not, or did not want to, go out back to the one-holer, probably 75 feet away behind the house. The "jar" was about like a ten-quart pail with a wire bail or handle. It flanged out so you could sit on it for number 2. First of all, it was quite heavy for a little boy like me. As a grownup, you would just take it in one hand and walk with it. It was always overfull, so you had to be very careful not to spill it. It was always pretty ripe, because it would have several days supply in it. But, for me to carry it, I would have to straddle it and with two hands take baby steps so as not to get any of it on me or spill it in the house. Then, it would be taken out back, not always to the back (out) house, but on the ground anywhere off the path to the back house.

I stuttered badly until I was about 13, worse than I have ever seen in all my years. I just could not start anything without stuttering. It was awful and embarrassing and even worse when my mother would slap me across the face when I did stutter. Another habit I had was uncontrollable laughing. Just nerves, I think, but I would laugh without being able to stop. A good slap across the face did help, though, or at least my mother thought so.

My mother had complete power over us kids and she could go from happy to almost abusive in a very short time. My brother Tommy never forgot her mood swings. One Christmas he saved his money and bought her a watch. She got mad at him about something and broke it right in front of him. One time when she caught him stealing a pack of her cigarettes, she took four of them back and left him the other two, saying, "Let's share. It's been a long winter. Don't let your father know."

If my mother were alive, she would deny all the things I have said. I am sure of it. But my sister and brothers say the same thing. Looking back, maybe I was not as nice as I should have been. Who knows?

She never asked for anything, never seemed to wish for anything. I did not once hear her say she would like new curtains, a washing machine, or anything a wife would normally want. She was a crossword puzzle fan, and she drank a lot. She always sat with her left leg bent under her, and she would sit there at the table most all day, every day, doing crossword puzzles and drinking beer. She never drank when she was young, though. I was probably about ten when she started. It was when my father became constable of the town and he had to go and keep order at the dances they held over at the grange hall. She went with him and although he never, ever danced, she would dance every one. She loved it. So she started going out. We kids were getting older, and it gave her a freedom she never had before. A summer couple would pick her up to go play *Beano*. My father never took her. My parents would play poker at least once a week with different people in town and they all drank. I was the oldest and got the "privilege" of babysitting the younger kids.

My mother tried to leave home once. She and my father had a bad argument and she said she was leaving him and us kids. She started walking to Ellsworth and intended to get to Bangor with my uncle who drove a mail truck every day from Ellsworth to Bangor. She knew that she could stay with relatives in Bangor until she could figure out what she was going to do. My sister, Sandra, remembered her standing by the kitchen sink, looking out the window and just crying. It had to have disturbed her to remember it after all these years. Thinking back, my father did not lose many arguments and my mother had to obey him. He eventually got into his car and found her somewhere between our house and Ellsworth, and brought her back. I said that my mother did not ever ask for things that would have made her life easier, yet, he always collected bottles, coins, and spent untold dollars on his stamp collection. Probably he was a selfish man. The more I think about things and read what I have written, I have to think that all the members of my family – my three brothers and my only sister, Sandra, could each write a book about their life growing up in our home. Being older gave me an earlier look at things. Financially, things were better when I got a little older, but by that time, I was not home anymore. I moved out after the 7th grade, so that in itself had to have helped some.

My mother and father were coming home from the Surry dance one night and they stopped on top of the hill a few miles from our house. Daddy stood on the running board of the truck to pee. A car came up the hill speeding and sideswiped the truck. It totaled the side of the truck and dropped Daddy on the road behind the truck. He was mostly drunk. The state cop was obviously going to show up, so he had someone bring him home. It was around one in the morning and I was up. He came in under his own power and sat at the table. He asked me to open a beer for him. He wanted to be drinking a beer in his own home when the state cop came, so when he smelled of alcohol it would fool the cop. He was shaking all over.

Everyone was drunk a lot. No money, but always enough for booze and butts. They did roll their own sometimes and I even did it for them. I never drank much, and I **never** smoked a cigarette. I always hated it.

Around the late 40's they got into this fad of using the cigarette holder. They were long and you would put the cigarette into the end and smoke it that way. If you ever saw photos of President Roosevelt, he always had them and they became the rage. Can you imagine? Dirt poor and imitating the president? When I think about it, we must have been the laughing stock of the town.

My mother was prejudiced. She was part Native American Indian but she would never admit it. She would say, "The only good Indian is a dead Indian." She said that a lot and she said the same thing about African Americans.

Cod fish

We often had what we called "slack fish" to chew on. It was cheap, of course; otherwise we would not have had it. Actually it was a whole cod fish that had been left outdoors on a drying rack and heavily salted. Hopefully it would preserve the fish from rotting and for the most part, it did. When it came to us, it was a whole fish that was split apart and flattened out. It just lay around from the kitchen table to the sideboard, generally staying in the kitchen area. Remember, the kitchen was our "great room" for everything from entertaining to playing checkers. Anything that went on went on in the kitchen. Deer that were shot would sometimes be put right on the table and cut up. We would pack smelts in boxes on the kitchen floor. The whole room was only about 12 by 12 feet. Put in the wood stove, an old black cast iron sink, a table, a couple of homemade benches for kids to sit on, and two chairs for each end of the table for my father and mother to sit on, and don't forget the wood box. That room was pretty well filled up.

Well, anyway, my mother would use some of the fish to make cod and gravy. She chopped up pieces and made white gravy with egg in it sometimes. We always liked it. It was tasty. Still, digging my fingers into the dried cod, stripping a piece off, and just chewing it was the best for me! It would lie around for a long time and everybody picked at it. The problem was, at the deeper part of the fish where the salt could not soak through, there would be maggots living. It was a fine line to get as close to the rotten flesh and not get a maggot. You see, nobody wanted to throw it away because there was always just a little bit you could still pick off. Everyone in the house picked at it with their fingers, and washing your hands before touching food was not something we ever thought about.

One summer my father got a hold of some fresh cod. He put chicken wire across a couple of saw horses and tried to salt and dry the fish. It lay outdoors all that summer. Flies were always on them and I suppose they got eaten at some point, but that was the last time he tried that. I am sure there were plenty of maggots in his fish.

Russell and Dorathy (pregnant with Sandra,) with David, (Robert's cousin,) Robert, (front left,) and Tommy.

A sense of humor

I get a lot of my characteristics from my father. I can joke and laugh off a lot of problems. I know sometimes that irritates your mother, but she will take something too serious and store it up. If you can't do anything about a situation right now, then make the most of it. I have had plenty of times that I had to hide my reactions and humor has helped. I have seen my father on death's door, and he would joke about it. He had Sandra and me laughing just hours before he died. I have seen him hurt very badly and not be able to work for weeks at a time and he would joke about it. One time when he was laid up for weeks, I had to go out to the clothesline to get him his long johns. It was very cold and they were frozen stiff. I mean, you could hold them right out and they did not droop! I brought them in and he said, "Look at that! That is how I will be brought in some day." My father could be a real pain in the ass, but he always had a good sense of humor.

He was just coming out of the woods from hunting (illegally, by the way) and before he got to the road, he heard a car coming so he stayed back out of sight. The car stopped right in front of him, though they could not see him. They were just stopping to dump their garbage along the side of the road. My father knew who they were. After they drove away, he picked up all the garbage and kept it for months. He waited until they were gone from their house, and then he dumped it all over their yard.

In the evening before he went to bed, he would go to the door step to pee, as we all did, but he had his own little ritual. Behind our house about a mile was the East Blue Hill Road, and on it lived Hildred, an old spinster. I am not sure if my father even knew her, and I certainly don't think she could have heard him, but he would holler as loud as he could, "Hey Hildred! I am getting ready to take it out now. Hey Hildred, I'm starting to p--- now. Hey Hildred, I am almost done now. I am getting ready to shake it. Better hurry, Hildred. I am getting ready to put it away now. Too late now Hildred! Maybe next time." Every night he went through the same spiel. That was the kind of humor I grew up with. Most everything had a sexual tone. My mother did not have a good sense of humor but she always had a dirty mind. No jokes, but always dirty-minded.

Sometimes he would take a can of spray paint and walk around the field and paint just a couple of flowers or field daisies – some bright florescent color. From the road, people would stop and stare, not knowing what to think. He really was artistic. He painted rocks, shells, toilet walls, and even his stove chimney. He was always drawing boats on pieces of boards and such.

My father loved things that made noise, like cherry bombs or dynamite. There was a time when anybody could go into a hardware store and buy sticks of dynamite. You would need a fuse wire to light it, and this would take some time to burn to the stick and that was how you timed it. I have done it myself. As the wick burned, it would get to the stick and set off the charge by a fuse cap that would be crimped onto the fuse wire by simply slipping it onto the fuse. You crimped it with your teeth. Not as dangerous as you might think.

I grew up with dynamite. A small part of a stick would blow up a stump. Thinking back, I guess it was not very smart to allow it to be handled by a child, but my father even carried it under the seat of his truck. Before the advent of digger trucks and back hoes and ways to break up the earth, it was a common thing to have around.

Being the oldest gave me some perks, some status, and I think my father was proud of me. I was the first to use a rifle and the first to go hunting with my father. I usually had first-hand knowledge of just about everything, even the dynamite. I knew how to blow a stump at about the age of ten. Who else can say that? Ha! Name someone. He would let me stand beside the target up in the field when he was target practicing. I'll tell you how this worked: It was about 300 feet away and he had a target set up next to the garden. I would stand next to it, maybe ten feet. He would shoot and I would holler down to tell him where he hit. Then I would put a piece of grass or a stick or something to plug the bullet hole and wait for him to shoot again.

Funny, even when very young, I knew every dollar my father owed. Kids today might have some idea, but not the whole story. I have a lot of my father's old diaries and journals where he kept track of work he did and payments he received. Course, the house was small, so nothing escaped my attention.

Another thing, when filling the wood box, I would try to bring as large a load of wood in my arms as possible. If we had company he would say, "Look at the lazy bastard – taking a big armful so he won't have to go get another one." That was praise. He meant to say it like that and it was fine with me.

I never called my father, "Dad," always "Daddy," but when I was older, I would sometimes wait to get his attention without addressing him so I wouldn't have to call him "Daddy."

Robert's father, Russell Stevens, center, with brothers, "Big Red," left, and Morris Jr. on his right, with Sandra and Wesley. Behind them is a 1928 Chevrolet. c. 1949.

Big Red

My father's brother, Maurice, the one they called Big Red, stayed with us many times. When he was a young man, he lived in Massachusetts. After his father's death at the age of 42, he helped to support his mother, Amanda, and his siblings. Amanda was an accomplished organist who played for the Methodist church in Ballardvale and Red would pump the organ for her. (When Amanda got pregnant by Ken Kibbee, whose wife was also pregnant, the two families moved to Ohio, probably because of the scandal that would have ensued.) According to his daughter, Betty Ann, he met her mother at that church.

For the first 14 years after Big Red was married, he was an almost perfect husband and father, a good provider who doted on his two children. He had green houses, did stained glass work, interior decorating, house painting, and other things in demand. He was a very talented man. When he left them for another woman and abandoned them completely, it was devastating to Betty Ann.

During the time I was growing up he would come to visit, usually when he was down and out. On those occasions he would work with my father painting or doing other odd jobs for the summer people until he could get back to Massachusetts. He always liked coming to Maine, but did not want anyone to know he was from here. He even had an accent to prove he wasn't a Mainer – sort of an Irish lilt that he worked on.

He became a heavy drinker and was addicted to cigarettes. The last time I saw him was at my father's house. He had a hole in his throat and a voice machine he tried to talk with. He kept smoking after they put a hole in his throat - just put the cigarette in the hole, then put the voice machine back in the hole when he wanted to say something. Sure was something to see, a first for me. He was pretty much on his way out by that time. He died in Massachusetts and is buried in a pauper's grave with a gravestone marked only by the letter "H."

When the bay froze over

During the winter months there was not a lot of work for anyone, and smelting was something a lot of men did. The fish ran in huge schools and they were caught through the ice in the frozen bays along the coast. The fishing tents, constructed on sleds, were homemade and generally looked alike. They were simply made and most men owned at least two tents.

You began with a platform with a hole in the ice floor about one foot wide the entire width of the tent. It was framed up with cedar or pine sticks approximately one inch square. Everything would be covered up with a light canvas and then painted, being careful not to leave even a pin hole where light could come through. A small stove would be made out of a five-gallon pail with a three or four-inch chimney out the roof. It would only hold four or five-inch pieces of wood. From one side to the other at the top of the hole was a wooden bar that was hung with two strips of rubber from an old tire tube so the bar could be hung - and lines, five of them, across the bar and dropped into the water. The hole on the floor of the tent would be about one foot by five feet. The hole in the ice would be cut first and the tent moved over it. It was possible to get several bushels of smelts at every tide. The fish would not always be there. They came in with the tide and there would be good days and bad days, but if they were running, they were very thick, and my father always got more than his share.

My father was a fisherman, as was his father. When the bay froze over in the winter, he always did well – so well, in fact, that he would not bring all the fish off the ice until after dark. After the smelts were packed in ice in boxes, they were left by the side of the road and a freight driver who drove through Surry every day would pick them up.

My father would bring some when the other fishermen came off the ice, and then later when no one would notice, he would bring the rest. I suppose he took them over to Ellsworth or some other freight pickup. I never understood why he didn't just take all the smelts off at once, but I didn't think too much about it at the time. He was probably making more money than the other fishermen, but it sure did not help us out too much as a family. The grocery bill at the little store in Surry was always behind.

When I got older, I found out why he and my uncle Red got a better catch. The legal, proper way to fish for smelts, and the way everyone else was fishing, was to tie lines from their tents with heavy sinkers (usually five) to a rod slung from old pieces of inner tubes to give it a spring effect to jiggle the lines.

When my father and Red got to their tent, they pulled the lines up and used what they called a "magee." Sounds like a crazy name, and I have no idea where they dreamed it up, but those two had a name for everyone in Surry, so who knows what inspired the name "magee." Eventually I got involved in helping to make a "magee" and was taught how to use it. The "magee" started with a rifle-cleaning rod for a small arm like a .22 caliber. A darning needle was soldered onto the end of it and then two wires from a coat hanger were soldered onto the sides of the rod and then bent in a fashion to make a spear. A string was tied to the end so it could loop around the wrist and not get lost in the water. It was easy to use. Just spear the fish and with a quick jerk, the fish would be in the slat box and the next would be speared. It was a lot faster than getting them on a line and taking them off. Every fish would be speared, and it left a very small hole that could not be seen unless you looked very closely. If the fish were not very thick or were not biting for some reason, then spearing got you the fish.

There were several reasons why the fish may not be biting. Perhaps bigger fish were chasing them. If the tide was not running strong enough or perhaps the brooks that ran into the bay were not flowing fast enough to bring food into the bay. With the spear, it was most certainly a way to get fish when nobody else could get them. The problem was you could not bring 100 lbs of smelts off the ice when all the other smelters got hardly anything.

Just like today, we have certain seasons when it is just fly fishing or dip net fishing or only fishing in brooks. Using the "magee" was illegal and they were very secretive about it. It seems that their father also had a spear for fishing, not designed just like theirs, but it was probably where they got the idea. I don't know what would have happened if I had told, but it was never a problem. I would not have told anyone. Even when my father was old, I brought up the subject of the "magee," and he was very sensitive about it. Pride, maybe. He said it was up in the attic but I never found it. I am sure Red got rid of his, because I never saw one again. It was obvious they were both scared of getting caught doing something illegal, which probably would not have been as bad as everyone in Surry finding out about it.

Never did shoot a moose

After dark one night, my father heard what he thought was a moose. It was quite a ways out behind the house and he was making a noise, calling to his girlfriend I guess. My father started calling back to him as loud as he could, but that wasn't good enough, so he took an old magazine, rolled it up, and started to call with that. It worked. He had the moose answering him. Well, he didn't just want to talk to that moose, he wanted to kill him. He couldn't do that with the moose at least a thousand feet out in the woods.

He handed me the magazine and had me keep calling. He got his gun and a flashlight and headed out into the woods to try and get close enough to the moose to shoot him. I began to call and got him answering me, but my father never did get him. The moose would have been jumpy and nervous anyway, and probably mistrusted my call. Being young, I wasn't timing it right or it was too loud. I guess our voices through that rolled-up magazine didn't quite sound like his girlfriend. Who knows, but it was an experience I didn't forget.

Another time when I was about nine or ten years old, someone said to my father, "You know there is a moose in the field down the road." It was the middle of the day. We headed down and saw it standing in the field in a narrow spot where the field opened up below him. We ditched the car behind a cottage and walked back through the woods to where the moose was. My father was coaching me to stay behind a tree in case he charged us. We were about 50 yards from him and my father was about to drop him when a car came by and stopped to stare at the moose. There was always more traffic when summer people were in town, so as soon as that car left, another showed up. After a couple more, he decided it was too risky. Too many people knew about the moose and it would not be easy to get it taken care of before someone else came along. There could have been an investigation by the wardens and they probably would have come to our house first. My father did have a reputation with them.

Several times they tried to trip him up. One time when he was coming out of the woods at night, two wardens shined the lights right on him. When they checked him over, he had a gun and a light, but no shells for the gun. They asked him where the shells were and he said, "I hid them." They were not very happy, but what could they do? He would never be caught with all three. I don't know now if he could get away with that trick. They have tightened up on the gun and hunting laws.

He never did shoot a moose. There just weren't that many down on the Neck.

My uncle Chippy shot a moose once (illegally,) and had it all cut up and packaged. He actually gave a lot of it away and we got some of it ourselves. Still, most of it ended up in his freezer. He hadn't eaten any yet. He got a call one night and somebody told him that the wardens were heading up to his house because someone had tipped them off that he had shot a moose. Well, Chippy panicked and unloaded his freezer into his boat. He lived right on Graham Lake, so he rowed out on the lake and dumped every last piece. Nobody ever showed up. He never got a shred of that moose meat.

The man was mortified

When I was ten, my father and I were working in the woods and the tractor needed to be cranked. He was cranking when it back-fired and broke his arm. He held his arm out to me, lifted his hand up, and it dropped back down. He said, "----! I broke it!" He told me to turn the gas off on the tractor and he started back to the house. I shut it off. It was a home-made tractor from a Ford Model "A." It had a gravity feed gas tank and it would drip dry if not turned off. It was shut off at the sediment bulb. No starter - just a hand crank. I ran to catch up with him. We walked into the house together where my mother was frying deer meat at the wood stove in her shorts and bra. It was summer, and the house was very hot. The door and windows were all open. She turned around and said, "What happened to you, you old bastard?" He said, "I broke my arm."

We had no car at the time, so he and my mother started walking to the Blue Hill hospital, about ten miles away. They walked quite a ways when a man up the road stopped them to talk. After talking a while, he asked them where they were walking to. When my father told him he had just broken his arm, the man was mortified. He took them to the hospital and to all the follow-up visits. It was a nice thing to do and I am sure it gave him something to talk about with his rich summer friends. His name was Mr. Blood.

Wesley, Tommy, Walter, and Sandra, with their mother, Dorathy. Behind them is the house with the crawl space attic where Robert slept, and the 1936 Plymouth that he drove down the Neck and had to get towed back.

Wesley

Wesley was low man on the totem pole in the family. He was born at home after three days labor. One day when he was four years old, my father was hauling gravel from the beach across the road using the horse and wagon. The wagon had rubber tires like on your car. He was coming up the hill from the beach and the horse was doing all he could do, so my father was slapping his rump and hollering at him to get going. All of us kids were running alongside the wagon keeping up, and Wesley got too close to one wheel and it caught him and knocked him down and rolled up one leg and up his body.

When my father noticed and stopped the horse, the wheel was right on Wesley's head. I was close by, within a couple of feet. My father could do nothing but slap the horse and roll the tire off his head. Wesley was in the hospital for weeks and he had to learn to walk all over again. He was just a little slower than the rest of us kids, but he read a lot and was really good at remembering radio jingles and other things that I could never remember. He was called names by both of my parents – terrible, filthy names. (Actually my mother called me the same filthy names.) They would ask him to do something and if he hesitated for just an instant, they would say, "You stupid son of a -----! Robert, go get that." I was naturally quick and responded quickly when my father hollered. Wesley never stood a chance.

My Uncle Red was at our house one day and said to my mother and father, "You have the stupidest ---- for a son I have ever seen. Hope you don't mind my saying so." My mother said, "No, no, no. He is stupid. Don't mind at all." Another time someone said, "Wesley is your boy, isn't he?" and my mother said, "Yes, ashamed to say it, but I guess we have to claim him." Both times Wesley could hear every word they said about him. Long after he got out of the army, Uncle Red apologized to him, something my father would never do. Red was a kinder person.

Wesley was always a hard worker and never went very long without a job, although he mostly had work that required a lot of physical labor. He was even able to retire with some benefits. He told me he was the black sheep of the family. My father and mother always made fun and ridiculed him. I don't really remember, but Sandy and I wonder if maybe we did too.

Always getting hurt

One thing about my father was that he was not willing to take the blame for anything. No matter what happened, it was always someone else's fault. When he fell off a roof, it was because the staging was not installed right. When he got picked up for drunk driving, it was because the person with him said he wouldn't drive, and my father was forced to do it. When he got hung by his rump and did not work for many weeks, it was because the man driving the tractor jerked it and my father could not hold on. When he got run over with his own tractor, it was because one of the kids must have put the gearshift into low gear when playing on it. When he got into the bad car accident with Uncle Fudd and Aunt Betty and spent weeks in the hospital, it was all because Fudd did not change the tires on his car before going on a long trip.

Boy, I cannot count the times my father was laid up. He was always getting hurt, and that kept him from working for weeks at a time. I could go on for hours with stories like this. It was *really something* that he lived to be 87! He often told us he was going to die at age 42 (like his father) or that he was "born to be hung."

As a young man living in Massachusetts, he was sliding on the snow and a big Buick ran over him. It even broke the bottle in his hip pocket. (The fact that he was drinking probably had nothing to do with it.) He spent some time in the hospital for that one, too.

When he was working in Bath, Maine, he fell on what they called a Marlin Spike. It was a tapered bolt or spike about six or eight inches long. It was attached to a tractor – just like a ball to a trailer hitch. They would drop a large plate of metal on it and haul it into place where it could be welded on a ship. Well, my father was standing on the back of the tractor riding to where the metal had to be picked up, when (according to him), the tractor driver jerked and he fell onto that spike. He always blamed the driver for this, as I've told you before, nothing was ever his fault. He was impaled on the spike and it took several men to lift him off of it. It jabbed into his rump. My mother had to pack the wound every day with gauze.

One time he was cutting wood with his brother, Red. My father was the axe man. Red would cut the tree down and he would limb the tree with the axe. Again, this was before chain saws were being used, so it was a continuous swinging and cutting all day. Accidents happen. He cut right down onto the top of his foot and it took 90 stitches to put it together. That is a lot of stitches! It split his foot between the toes and through to the bottom.

Once he dove off a rock down at the shore, struck his tooth, and broke it. He sat on the running board of the car and gradually pulled his tooth out. It took him a while and it must have hurt! He was one tough man.

Let me tell you about the car accident in Connecticut with my Uncle Fudd, his wife, Betty (Sidney was her real name,) and my mother. Uncle Fudd's tire blew, and the car went out of control and turned over. When they started counting, my father was not there. They figured he had wandered off in a daze but actually he went through the windshield, hit a guard rail, and fell 40 feet down an embankment. He was pretty well stove up and stayed in a Connecticut hospital for several weeks. When they were about to release him to a hospital in Bangor, closer to home, the nurse asked him what he was going to do when he got home. "Well," my father said, "I am going back to my spaghetti farm." When she asked him how to raise spaghetti, he knew he had her. He said, "Well, it's grown a lot like macaroni." He went into great detail about what had to be done to grow spaghetti and macaroni. She went off and must have told someone about what he said, because she came right back and said, "Mr. Stevens, I ought to kill you for that!"

We would eat them

We had hens at different times and if they did not lay eggs, we would eat them. Usually it was my job to kill them. If you ran up to a chicken and got above them, they would almost always squat down and stop. You would have to quickly grab the hen's two legs and the very ends of their wings, otherwise they flapped their wings and you couldn't hold them down. The chicken had to be right side up. Then you would lay the head and breast on the chopping block and generally they would stick their neck out enough to get a good swing with the axe. You didn't want to miss. Part of their head would stay on and it created some grief. It was best to hold the hen with your left hand and cut the head off with your right.

Then you would just throw them off to one side and let them flop around until they lay still. Just nerves, I guess, because they have no head left. Next came the messy part. They would have to be gutted out and if that was not bad enough, the feathers would have to be pulled out. We would lug enough water from the well to fill a wash tub and then heat the water on the kitchen stove, as hot as we could get it. The hotter the water, the better the feathers came off. The pin feathers were the worst. Sometimes they could be burned off. A piece of newspaper rolled up and set afire would do it. I did not like doing that job.

That is what we did

Before I was old enough to use a gun, I was taught to snare rabbits. It was really easy. You would find out where they traveled, usually in a thick brushy area. You would secure a stick to two trees by tying it, then you would hang a wire noose so that when the rabbit came, he would get his neck into it and strangle. It was common to do that. We didn't worry then, about properly draining the blood. After the rabbit was caught, it would be hung maybe from the limb of a tree and cut around the neck area. The hide would peel off of him just like a glove – unlike any other animal. At the time, I did not like it, but that is what we did. Now I almost go off the road for a chipmunk.

Preserving

Preserving eggs was something we did when I was young. We packed them in crocks or large jars with a mixture called "water glass."[1] This was probably not the correct term, but what everyone called it. We did not cook them first, just put them in the jars with the mixture.

Corned meat was another staple – always deer meat for us. There would be a layer of meat and salt, then another layer of meat and salt. It just prolonged the use of the meat we had.

Any jam or jelly we put up was without jar covers. We poured hot wax on the top of the jam, and then when we wanted to eat it we would just dig the wax out and start eating. The mold would be scraped off first, of course.

---

[1] Popular in the days of pre-refrigeration, this was actually a chemical called sodium silicate. It was sold in small tins and would be dissolved into water. The end result was a solution which would effectively seal the pores of the eggs, keeping out oxygen and moisture and prevent spoiling. Fresh eggs could be kept for up to one year.

I would have died

My father often peddled deer meat from the family car to customers in Ellsworth. We kids would be in the car with a wash tub full of deer meat. After he sold it, he and my mother would stop at Eddie Bond's, a beer joint, and we would be left in the car a long time waiting for them. Usually one of us had to go in to get my parents and tell them we were out of control in the car. We used to really fight and argue a lot in the back seat. You can't leave five kids in a back seat and expect them to be like angels.

One night we were in Ellsworth on one of our deer meat selling trips. I must have been about ten years old. My father met someone from Blue Hill who needed a ride home from Eddie's bar. Our car was an old 1932 Chevrolet and was not very tight. The muffler was gone. By the time we got to Surry my father decided he did not have enough gas to take the guy all the way to Blue Hill so he let him off where we turned onto the Newberry Neck Road.

When we got home and in the yard, my mother turned around in her seat, telling me to get out and get in the house. I could hear her and see her but I couldn't move. She told me again to get out, and when I did not move, she leaned over and slapped me in the face. It didn't hurt and I remember thinking it was funny (ha ha,) that it was the first time I have been hit and it not hurt.

They realized then that I was asphyxiated from the exhaust fumes. They lugged me into the house and laid me on the bed and gave me some tea. It wasn't very long before I revived, but had my father gone on to Blue Hill with that man, I would have died in the back seat.

He shot a lot of deer

When my father shot a deer, it would hang for a long time in the shed or behind the house in a tree. When I would cut off some for my mother to cook, blow flies would be on it and we had to shoo them away. We had to cut off the dried-up flesh on the surface to get rid of the fly droppings and the dried crust of meat where it hardened, be we never got sick from eating it.

He shot a lot of deer. One fall he killed sixteen of them. I must have been around eight or nine that year. We ate a lot of that deer meat, but he sold most of them. Forest C., the game inspector at the Surry store would tell out-of-state hunters who did not get a deer that he knew someone who would sell them one. They would go to my father and pay him $35 for the deer. When they went back to the Surry store to have it tagged, Forest would know that my father owed him $10. That I do remember.

If he thought someone was squealing on him about deer hunting, he would gut out a deer and deposit the innards of the carcass on their doorstep when they were not at home. It they went off the Neck he knew it. We were his spies. Every night when he got home, one of the first things he would ask us was, "Anybody go down the Neck today? Who was it? How many in the car? Did they come back up? Same people in the car?" My father kept track of all of that. That road was pretty much his territory, and if there were any wardens or authorities that he felt could be on to him, he wanted to know. He did not want anyone staying on the Neck that could catch him at anything.

My father had a lot of places that he hunted, but always on the Neck. He did not trust any other place to hunt because he did not have any control as to what went on anywhere else. I mentioned that in most of the areas he hunted he had a deer stand of some sort in a tree. Nowadays when hunters think of deer stands, they are thinking about an apparatus that hooks to a tree and sometimes you can climb a tree with it – like a staging bracket lift. It will have a nice place to sit and sometimes a shelter of some kind to keep the weather out. Pretty fancy. Well, let me tell you something. There was nothing fancy with my father's stands. They were just a way to get up in the tree. Most times the limbs were what you climbed up on, and sometimes it would be a few pieces of boards nailed to the side of the tree to get you up to the lowest limb. A piece of rope would be used to haul your gun up, and maybe a sleeping bag. The rope could be used to tie yourself to the tree so if you fell asleep, you wouldn't fall out. This is sort of beating around the bush some, but I kinda wanted to explain that hunting from a tree was not always what it was cracked up to be.

It would be dark. Apples were spread around below the tree, usually in a nearby brush pile. Deer could smell them but a warden could not see them. Another reason for the brush pile was at dark when everything was quiet, any deer getting into the brush pile would make noise enough to wake you up when they started eating. Back to the story: One night my father turned the light on and there stood a good-sized deer. Well, he had a shot gun and a few shells in his pocket, but because he had not loaded it until getting up in the tree, by mistake he put a shot of birdshot in the chamber. When he shot the deer, it did not move, just stood there. As my father started down the tree, the other shells fell out of his pocket. Well, after he got out of the tree and on the ground, the deer was still standing right there and not moving. He frantically looked for the shells that had fallen but they were in the brush and he couldn't find them. He needed them to kill the deer. He walked over to the deer and saw that it had been hit in the face and was bleeding but it did not look like he would die. The deer began walking away and my father followed him. After a while he put his hand on the deer's back and kept looking for something to hit the deer with and kill him. No matter how much he looked as they kept moving along, he couldn't find anything big or heavy enough. He finally let the deer move off and he came home and told us what had happened.

Months later during hunting season, he was driving toward town and saw a deer that someone had shot and it was hanging up. He stopped immediately and hollered out to the men, "Hey! That's my deer!" It took them back a little and they were defensive. Without even getting close, he knew it was the one that he had shot with birdshot. Of course, he told them about what he had done and the face of the deer was all banged up, so there was no question about it. He lost the deer, but had a good story.

He had several deer stands that he built throughout the woods. If he was up a tree, he had an advantage over the wardens and he could hear the deer coming long before he could see them. I was 12, not any older. My father planned to leave me at one of his deer stands, and then he would go down the road to another stand about a mile away.

It was just before dark and I had never been in that area before. We hurried up a hill and the last thing my father said was, "Just go here, and then go there, and you will come out on the Newberry Neck Road." Sounded good, and in daylight it would have been fine.

I sat in the deer stand until just before it got dark and I could hear a deer coming. I had plenty of time to be ready for him. I had to twist around because he was coming out behind me. I had the rifle trained on him when he came out of the woods. He came into the clearing and I followed him around and watched him eat and take his time. I guess I was thinking it might be a better shot in a minute or something like that, but that deer was as safe as could be. If I had accidentally pulled the trigger I would have gotten him.

Funny thing was I got down out of the tree when the deer left and looked around. In the tree there was still a little light but not on the ground. I could not see anything. I started in the direction I thought was right and went quite a ways, but did not come out where I thought I should be. Now I was scared and stared hollering loudly. I made a lot of noise, and suddenly I was right where I knew I should be. I was feeling pretty stupid, but who would know, right? I was supposed to meet my father at Lenny Reynold's house about a mile down the road and when I arrived my father was already there. He asked me, "Was that you hollering?" "No, that wasn't me," I said. In the dark and silent night, I guess he heard someone making a noise. Wasn't me, though. Only you and I know for sure.

I'll tell you one thing I will remember as long as I live. It was my first time hunting. I was following my father and he had his .30 and I was following him with the 12-guage shot gun. We were just shy of entering a clearing and my father was pretty sure that there would be a deer in that spot. In a whisper he said, "Be ready now. I expect a deer to be in there." "Well," I whispered, "I'm ready. I got the hammer back already."

I was following him with the gun cocked and ready to fire. Any mishap and I would have cut him in half, as close as we were. Man, oh man! He just exploded! He was so mad I thought he was going to blow a gasket! He hollered so loud at me that any deer or anything else for a mile around could have heard him. It ruined that day for me. Did I learn a lesson? Yeah, I sure did.

A dead-end road

The road I grew up on was a dead-end road and no way to get off the Neck except going back the way you went down. There was a cross road just down from our house that took you to East Blue Hill but it could only be used a few weeks a year. It is a good road now, but back then it was not maintained. It was muddy in the spring and it was never plowed in the winter. The town had all it could do to keep the Neck plowed. In front of our house was a very bad spot, soupy and muddy in the springtime. The snow blew across that field so badly that the plow trucks could not get through and men would come down after the storm and hand shovel in front of the plow truck so it could finish the job of plowing. There was not much traffic on the road in those early days. My father parked the car right down next to the road. We never drove up our driveway all winter. It was never plowed. Everything was lugged up, about 300 feet. My father was not wild about shoveling, so we had only a packed-down footpath. It was always snow to walk through, or the mud. It was actually a field, so we could not expect much for a driveway. On that flat stretch down by the road, we could not coast the car to start it, so we would have someone come by to give us a tow in order to get it started. Hardly anyone ever drove down the Neck Road when I was young. There was a doctor's wife who came down from time to time, but other than that, most of the people who lived there year-round, including us, did not have a car that worked on a regular basis. My father did not have regular transportation until he began working for Union River Telephone Company. I was 15 and already living away from home, so did not get much benefit from that.

Just as you started down the road from Surry Village there was another low, bad spot for about 300 feet that got so muddy, cars usually could not get through without getting in the mud and pushing and prying up a tire and throwing gravel or anything under the tires to get out.

We were just getting past that spot once when the steering wheel came right off in my father's hand. We were not going very fast. He just held it over towards my mother and said,

"Hey, Dot, look at this. No steering wheel." I told you we did not have much for cars.

We bought cars for $15 and up, so as you can see, they were not worth anything. My father never borrowed much money. We did not have any way to pay it back, but sometimes just before school started, he might go to the bank and borrow $200. With that, we got school clothes and a new car. We would be starting with a clean slate with the Surry store also.

I hated it when I had to go to the store and get something on credit and they refused me. I would go back home and my father and mother would curse the store keeper for being a "cheap son of a -----." It was not pleasant. It seemed being the oldest, I was asked to do things that a small boy should not have to do. If we needed a chain fall, a device to lift something like a motor, I would be driven to Jappie Carter's house and had to go inside to ask. Sometimes we got it and sometimes we didn't. So, work on the car might have to wait while my father figured out some other way to get the job done.

During the time I grew up on Newberry Neck, there were some unique characters that became a part of my life. "Fingers" was a guy that had unusually long fingers. That by itself might have given him the nickname, but his hands were always dirty. I don't think he ever washed them. Boy, when you get a nickname in a small town, it sticks.

George Elmer "Shag-nasty, Piss to the Windward" K. was a local storekeeper that never washed his hands either. There was no bathroom or water in the store, so when he had to relieve himself, he just went out the back door (and probably into the wind sometimes.) Then he would be back in the store doling out cheese and other products that were not prepackaged at the time.

Regina, or "Screaming Genna," as my father always called her, was always hollering to her husband. My father had another name for her, "Old one tit." She had had cancer or something and one breast was gone. I did not understand at the time and I would always try to see which one was gone. My mother and father thought she was below us (in social standards.) Can you imagine that?

Irene (Young) Buzzell and Sidney Moon were nice people who lived down the Neck. Sidney worked at odd jobs and also in the woods. Their daughter, Jean, was born the 16th of February and me on the 14th, so for years we celebrated our birthdays together – always at their house. My parents played cards with them. They had three children and we had five, so we got along well. During all the time I knew them, I don't remember them coming to our house. I liked all of them and have fond memories of the whole family. (Irene was a sister to Harvey Young. He was married to my Aunt Betty, father of my cousin, Philip. He was a drinker, and he burned to death in a house fire on the Neck.)

BoBo D. and his sister must have come from a poor family, though it didn't seem as if anyone had much in those days. They lived right next to the Surry Store – Carter's Store, owned by Forest and Esther Carter. To my father, he was "Fish head Carter." Remember, it was Esther who brought the oatmeal and flour to our family, left at the mailbox. She delivered the mail. Forest was the game inspector who sent folks to my father to buy the deer.

The D---- family was always lousy with head lice. Over and over again they would be sent home from school and the whole school would be checked over by Mrs. Dumphy, the school nurse. She was always sort of whistling, low, and she never stopped making that sound, letting air through her teeth. It's funny how you remember that sort of thing. We were sent home sometimes, quarantined for a week or so, but not for head lice. I don't remember why. I don't think I ever had head lice, but the treatment at our house was to wash the head with kerosene. It burned, but got rid of the lice.

The Carlisle family males were called "Big Gut," "Little Gut," and "Teeny Weenie Gut."

Then there was Artel McG. He was probably about my father's age and lived with his mother. Because they were heavy drinkers too, my father would often stop there. Artel stuttered quite badly and his intelligence was not too good. One time a bunch of guys were there and one of them spit on the floor. Artel said, "Dit-tit-tit-tit, don't spit-spit-spit on the floor, sssspit on-on-on the, the wall. Mamma-a, m-mama has to w-w-wash the floor.

"Plunger," was another character. He was given that nickname because he was walking across the ice in the bay and a lot of the other fishermen could see that if he went a little farther, he would fall off the ice. They hollered and hollered and sure enough, he walked right off the ice and went out of sight. Even so, he would not let go of the things he was carrying, and went back down a couple of times before they could get him out of there.

"Walk-in Slosh" was another man that was on the ice one winter and did almost the same thing as "Plunger." He was walking across the ice and he should not have been out there because the ice was breaking up and getting soft. Many guys were watching him when he walked into an ice hole that was cut out for a fish shack. They had to help him quickly because you only have a short time to survive in cold water.

I'll tell you about Phoebe and Emory Grindle. I remember being at their house. Their kids were close to our age, but all girls. I was about eight years old when Phoebe died and Emory had to bring up those girls by himself. It must have been very hard. I don't think he ever remarried. He lived next to the road on property that is now worth a million dollars, right on the beach. Annie and the Buzzell's also had property that is worth the same now. Beach front property was worth nothing then. I am sure they all sold their land for a song, got practically nothing for it. Most those folks died with nothing of value.

I actually owned a large plot of land on the Neck for some time but never did want to move back down there. It would be nice to see some of the OLD friends I used to have. I have really fond memories of some of them. They were all very nice to me and my family, regardless of my father's nicknames and prejudice of everyone. As nice as I am to anyone I meet, I still fight to overcome that deep-down tendency to look for their faults.

The thing I remember about all of them, as poor as they had to be, they all had a clean home and a car that always seemed to run. When their kids went to school with me, they had clothes that looked clean and good. There are other people I grew up with, but the Newberry Necker's were the ones I saw the most often because we didn't get off the Neck very much.

As a child, I had no idea of geography. I don't ever remember going to Bangor, and Ellsworth was seen only from the back seat of a car. I went to Blue Hill once and Deer Isle once. And get this – it was when the toll ticket taker was there in a little wooden building just before entering the bridge area. I don't know what prompted that trip, but it was quite a ride in an old car.

Out in the bay

One summer, a construction company moved a large house, the size of our farmhouse now, from High Street in Ellsworth, down Pine Street, and onto a barge. That was quite a task. It sat on a barge out in the bay for a week or more before it was moved to Blue Hill. It sure was funny to see a whole house out in the bay. It really stood out. It may have been no big deal to some, but it sure impressed me!

Something that stands out in my mind was the large sail boats that would come up the bay in front of our house. Huge, beautiful boats would come into Surry Bay and anchor there for days. It was the time of sailing, before motorized or jet boats, and people would come for the summer theater. Big name actors would be there. It was a beautiful sight to see those boats.

One year my father was given a sail boat, and I remember that it was quite good. He had been on the water a lot, so he thought he could sail it. Anyway, all seven of us started out, and the wind seemed to be blowing up the bay toward Surry Village, so going up was no problem. When we started back, that was when things got sticky. Anyone knowing about sailing would have tacked or whatever you call it, and brought us back. It was a pretty large boat and my father had to paddle it back. I don't remember any more trips in that boat. It either got sold or given to someone else.

Think back of pictures you must have seen of old work sailing boats. It was common to beach these vessels in a small cove to keep them safe until you wanted to get them out in the water and use them again. Anyway, I found one on the beach when I was walking around one time. It must have been 40 or 50 feet long and it was stuck in the mud of a small brook that ran into the bay. It was impressive. I got up on it and it really was something to see! This boat must have been 50 years old at the time and did not look like much, but it was all there and eventually my father helped the owner to get it floating again. I could sure imagine working on that boat. In my small world, it stood out in my mind, and I can still picture it. My father was a good worker and almost always available for small odd jobs that someone would want a day laborer for.

Winter Wooding

The fun part – winters. After talking to you and thinking about how we got the wood out in the winter, I remember we had terrible winters then, not like now. Winter wooding was different. First, the road to the wood had to be gotten ready and we had to cross a couple of small brooks. My father always cut the wood in four-foot lengths and would build the road as he went along. Across the swampy area he would build a corduroy bridge – just a simple affair with a couple of stringers and small logs run crossways on them to make a bridge – no nails or metals anywhere. It would always hold, unless we were dragging something that would lift up some of the logs, and then we would just put them back in place. As it started to freeze, brush would be laid in the road to freeze up and make a better base. We had several types of sleds. One was called a bunk. This was just a front set of sled runners which we would use to set the logs up high enough so the horse did not have to work as hard. We also used a sloven, which was a type of sled that was built by hewing out a couple of logs for runners and fastening them together to make a sled that could be dragged in bad conditions. It would only haul one half of a cord of wood, but it could get into any kind of area and get the wood out to the yard.

The most fun thing to use was actually two sleds chained together, one runner on the front chained to the opposite runner on the rear. When you turned, the front runner would go where you wanted to steer, and it would pull the rear runner to the right or left and get you around the corner. A horse could pull a couple of cords of wood, a lot of weight. It was fun to stand on the back runners and ride into the wood lot behind that horse. My feet would slip off the runners sometimes, but it was usually a slow, easy ride. While the sled was being loaded, it would freeze to the road, and there was no way the horse could start it moving, so he would pull to the left and to the right and finally the runners would break free.

Remember, if you move the front runners, the back ones move the other way. The sled had a center plank that could be let out so the sled could be brought closer for shorter lengths of wood, and let out for longer logs or wood. The whole experience was pleasant, not noisy like the equipment used today. I was small, but I did not want to miss anything.

One year we had a feller in Surry who took out our wood. His horse, named Dick, could count. He would ask the horse something needing a number and the horse would shake his head the required number of times. Boy, talk about being impressed! At that time, I had not yet seen the crow that Earl Stover had taught to talk, so having an animal show some intelligence was really something! Our animals did not last long enough to learn much. Mother Cat had kittens and we kept one of them, but all of us picked at it so much and would not leave it alone and eventually it died. It was just mauled to death. One or the other of the kids had it all the time and would fight over it and pull on it. It just could not mature. I guess it was love for the kitten, but the kitten died and we all knew why. Look at the picture of the kids by the house. Wesley is holding that kitten. That is the one that died and why it stands out in my mind is that most of our kittens were drowned. This one should have been also.

Danny Sexton, family friend, with Uncles Red and Irving Stevens, and Aunt Ruth Stevens

There was a mystery about Danny

Danny Sexton was a single man who lived a fourth of a mile away, making it an easy walk from our house. For many years I did not realize Danny had a connection to our family. He worked as a cook for a wood camp. It was common for a wooding operation to have a few shacks and a larger cabin for the men to eat and hang around in. This would be an area they planned to be in for a few years. Nowadays they would strip out the wood from the same area in a week or less with skidders.

In those days, Danny would go to work in the fall and not come out until spring. I am sure he did not drink on the job, but when he got out in the spring he would buy the summer supplies and then go on a bender that would last a long time or until he would go broke.

He lived in a little cabin, probably not any better than what he lived in all winter in the woods. Normally he was immaculate, but when he was drinking, he was very messy, and my father would visit him and try to keep him sober and cleaned up to some extent. I never saw him drunk. As his money got low, he would order a whole case of cooking vanilla. That is powerful stuff. He drank Sloan's liniment once, thinking it was vanilla, and got very sick. When he was sober, and he did stay sober for a long time, we kids would go visit Danny and he could sure make good doughnuts and cookies. I just remember being there and having his doughnuts. We did not get much of that kind of stuff. Years later, he moved up to Waltham to a logging camp and died there. I went with my father to visit him one time around 1955.

There was a mystery about Danny. I always wondered why my father took care of him and showed concern for him. I didn't find out until later that he had lived with my grandmother Amanda and was her boyfriend for years. Nobody talked about it then. My grandmother could not take the long drunken bouts, but they always stayed friends. I have some old letters from my grandmother given me by my Aunt Dot years ago. And now of course, it all makes sense. My grandmother had a lot of boyfriends. One was married at the time, and his wife and Amanda were pregnant at the same time. She moved to Ohio with them both and lived in their back yard in some sort of boxcar. (The result was Ruth Stevens.) I remember going to see my grandmother when she was working in Bar Harbor, and one time we brought her back to Surry so she could attend the Blue Hill Fair with us. I was 16 when she died, but I remember her well. My grandmother was neat. Nothing seemed to bother her. She fed her dog from the same fork she was eating from. One bite for her; one for the dog.

I would wake up in a sweat

I should tell you about my dreams. (Not like Dr. King.) I had the same one for many years, from age eight or nine until my teens, always the same. Picture yourself in water over your hips and trying to run. A person can only go so fast, no matter how hard he tries. Well, that was the problem in my dream.

There was a large ball, or round object like a ball. It was light in color and it was high, a lot taller than me. The thing was, it was always just behind me and about to run me over. I always stayed just ahead of it, but only by straining myself to the point of waking myself up. I knew that if I did not push myself, it would run me over and kill me. I would wake up in a sweat.

Quite a bind

One year during hunting season, I was sitting on the front porch of an old camp behind a house that had been empty for a while. The deer had been coming out into the field, over in a corner where there were a couple of apple trees. Those two trees had different kinds of apples on the ground underneath them. Normally we picked up apples, any kind, and put them down in the cellar of summer homes that my father kept care of.

It was about nine o'clock and had been dark for some time. I had been sitting there a while. It was quiet. I really liked the silence as much as anything else. I had to listen very carefully because the apples were not in a brush pile like usual and the deer could be right there and you could not hear them. What you did hear was the crunching of the apples when the deer bit into them.

Just about the time I was thinking of leaving to go back home, I heard a car coming up the old camp road. Man, the only place they could be going was right where I sat. Thinking they were just jacking deer and would flash the field and go, I quickly went behind the camp and hunched down, waiting for them to leave.

Well, they were not going. They were staying. They owned the camp. There were four of them. That put me in quite a bind. They all had guns and I had no way of knowing if they were gun shy or trigger happy. Seeing that I was night hunting, I had to think this one out, so I pulled an old "Daddy trick." I took the shells out of my gun and put them under the camp so I could get them later. With my gun and my light, I walked right out in front of them and said, "Hi!"

Well, they were surprised. I didn't know what to say then, so I just said, "How are you doing?" and walked out of there.

The old work horse

My father got a work horse when I was around seven or eight years old. I'm sure the horse was old when we got him and I can't imagine that it would have cost too much, seeing that my father didn't have much money. He arrived with a bunch of harnesses which the seller must have thrown in along with everything else he had for that horse. Daddy knew nothing about horses and tried for a long time to figure out how to harness him. He would have been better off with only one harness, but he had a bunch of leather and harness material that did not make sense to him. He eventually went down the Neck to Emery Grindle's home and asked Emery to come up and show him how to harness the horse.

I remember the old horse would crowd you against the stall if you were not careful. He would just lean against you and you could not move. I was small, of course, but the horse did not work at all unless I was tagging along. We had quite a bit of equipment, actually. Just for feeding him, we had to get hay and a mowing machine. It was all cast iron with two wheels. As it was pulled, it would run a cutter bar that sat off to one side about five feet long. For hauling hay, we had the old wagon that ran over Wesley when it was hauling beach stone. My father just built up the sides to haul the loose hay. I did not know anyone that had baled hay. Nowadays they have round bales that can sit outside without spoiling. We had to pitch it into the wagon, tread it down, pitch it up into the loft of our small barn, and tread it down again. It was a lot of work. We also had a single bottom plow, and I remember we did not use that as much. I don't know why. We never had much of a garden. I'm sure it would have come in handy.

Once we were out cutting wood, and the horse left the wood yard and went all the way to the house, about a half mile. I followed my father back home and there was the horse, grazing near the barn. My father tied the horse so he could not move and then beat him badly with a large board. The horse could not go anywhere, so he took quite a beating.

One day in early September, we were all going to the Blue Hill Fair. That was quite a thing for us kids. We never went anywhere. At the last minute, my father noticed the horse was out and grazing across the road. I was told to go get him and put him in the barn. I could not have been more than ten at the time. I got hold of his bridle and tried to lead him. I had both hands on the bridle, but the horse would pick his head up and fling me around. He liked it where he was and did not want to go to the barn. My father noticed and came down in the field to do it himself. That horse did not want to go in for my father either. Daddy got behind him, started with a rope and then began switching the horse on the rump so the horse began running. I was running alongside my father when the horse suddenly stopped and kicked back, hitting my father in the chest, sending him up in the air and down on his back. I began laughing so hard that I could not stand and was laughing while my father lay on the ground. Well, he got up, and because he was so furious, he ran the horse into the barn.

We loaded up for the fair and got there for most of an hour when my father had to go home because of pain. He had at least five broken ribs and he was out of work for a long time.

We had the horse for a few years and got a lot of work done with him. At that time, before chain saws, all wood was cut with a buck saw, and it could lay in the woods for a long time while you waited for someone with a team of horses to take it out for you. They were always getting backed up with haying or plowing or other work. We did not know anyone with a tractor. There just weren't any in our area. We could not get paid from the paper company until they had it in hand. As a side point, that was before de-barking was done at the mills, so all our logs had to be peeled of bark.

Henry Kane was the reason that my father bought a horse. Henry didn't get onto things like he should have. I think now, that he was a little lazy. His farm and building showed it. He ran the farm up the road near the watering trough. Water ran continuously and everyone got their water there, including us, because our well was always dry in the summer. Henry would promise to get our wood hauled out, but never got to it.

Back to the subject of deer

I remember the first deer I shot. I was 12. My father and I were going into a clearing and he told me to be ready because there was usually a deer there. Well, there was, but it was quite a way off, so to help me aim, my father let me steady the rifle on his shoulder. I got the deer, and we had to go down the Neck to see someone. It wasn't hunting season. Before going into the house we were visiting, he told me it would be better if he said he shot it, so that is what we did. After a while he said, "Actually, Robert shot it." They never did believe him, after what he had already said, so even though I had shot the deer myself, my first deer did not turn out to be a big deal after all.

I was involved in deer harvesting (sounds official!) from the time I was a very young boy. I would go out in the woods or in the shed where my father would have them strung up. Sometimes they would be hung in different locations, depending on how many he had shot. There could be as many as 15 in a matter of a few weeks. I told you he sold them, but he did not ever shoot them before the first of June. He wanted the fawns to be out on their own, and I guess they were by that time.

One night when I was around 12, give or take, we drove down the Neck and shined the light and saw two deer in a field. I was in the back seat and I shot the two deer. Then we went out to cut their throats and let them bleed. My father finished one, and then we moved to the other to do the same thing. I was holding the gun and the light and he reached down to cut the deer's throat but the deer was not dead by any standard and was getting up to go. My father got a hold of his horns and the deer was giving him a thrashing. I didn't know what to do to help him except to bring the gun up and down on the deer's head. That slowed the deer up so my father could cut his throat. The barrel was twisted because of how I hit the deer and he was very upset. "I would have got him anyway," he said. (It could not be his fault, right?) But I thought my father would be killed. What does a 12-year old kid know?

Usually, as soon as he shot the deer and dressed him out, he would reach up into it and remove the heart and liver. He would cut a stick right there to skewer them and bring them home. Within a couple of days we would eat that heart and liver. The heart we would cut up real thin and fry it and the liver we fried also, with onions. I might mention that I have not eaten heart or liver since I left home, but my father always loved to eat it even when he was not able to get it for himself. Then he would buy beef liver.

Sometimes, after the deer was cleaned, he would use rock salt and salt the meat down, layer by layer, in crocks. It would keep for months. Seems like there was always a way to do things without chemicals and refrigeration and other things we think we need today.

You may wonder what in the world did he do with all the deer hides. Well, that was simple. He had at least two hide dealers in the area. One was named Royce S. and he was on the Ellsworth Road. He would take a lot of the hides. Problem was though, Royce had to list someone's name for every deer that had been shot, so all of us kids and everyone that my father could think of, he would put down. To keep the hides from rotting, he would layer them and salt them heavily. They would last for a month.

There was also a fellow who came around once a year and he would take any amount of hides my father had, no questions asked. I think he paid three or four dollars for each one. He was an old Jew named Ikie. He drove an old panel truck and he traveled all around the county. He didn't just buy deer hides. He peddled produce and cheese and other things that could be sold.

That's something you don't see today. Those old peddlers sold an array of different products. Think about it. There was a man who came and sold ice, another sold *Ritz* dye, one sold *Argo* starch, and another sold *MendIts* for pans with holes in them. Two washers and a small bolt was what that consisted of. That saved a lot of old aluminum pots and pans. Maybe you remember the *Raleigh* man that sold household cleaning products and cooking things like vanilla and spices. How about the *Cushman* man that sold baked goods? Milk delivery was common, and of course the *Fuller Brush* man. *Electrolux* vacuums were common to sell in homes, and the same with sewing machines. It was just a different time, one we older folks miss sometimes.

Back to the subject of deer, we pretty much used everything. You know another thing, with all the deer he killed, he must have killed some trophy deer, I mean with a good set of horns, but he never did care about saving or mounting any of them. We never had stuffed animals or mounted heads.

When it came to hunting deer and the ways of getting it done, my father really was an expert. He went to great lengths to make things happen. He did not work full time, so he had time to try different things and see if they would work. For example, when he used a shot gun, he would take out all the pellets in the shell and tie them together. The reason he did that was so that after the gun was fired, the shell would spread apart into a large pattern. Maybe only a few pellets would hit the deer and it might not be enough to kill him. Now this was fine if you were shooting birds. Being spread out like that got you your bird. When he wanted the shots closer together to be sure and hit a deer, he would cut each pellet almost in half and crimp a piece of string into the shot, giving him the length of the spread. Makes sense, doesn't it?

At night, or any other time actually, if you hear one shot, it is very difficult to pinpoint where it came from. When a second shot is fired, instantly a person, particularly a warden, will know where it originated. So you can see how important it is to get a deer, especially at night, with only one shot. You just don't dare to shoot twice.

He was careful not to have bullets in his gun when he came out of the woods, and if he had a gun and a flashlight coming out of the woods at night, he would hide the bullets in a stump or culvert, or someplace he could get them better. You could not be arrested for night hunting without bullets. He was quite crafty on other things also, He would leave a blade of grass or a little slip of paper in a door and he would know someone had been there if it was missing. He also put his gas cap on tight, then turned it back a little so if someone took it off, he would know it. Anybody would naturally put it back on all the way, not knowing his trick.

My father always wanted to make a silencer. He kept at it but never did accomplish it with any efficiency. He tried about everything – stacked up washers on the end of the barrel, baby bottle nipples, anything he thought would cut down on the muzzle blast.

Once he tied a shot gun to a tree with a string attached, so when a deer passed, it would trip the trigger and be killed. It bothered him quite a bit, though, and he never tried that again. He was worried someone might walk into it and set it off. And it would have been just the right height to kill a man if he got tangled up in it. Another thing he did a lot was cut the end of the bullet so when it hit the deer it would mushroom quicker than normal, just for stopping power. As I have said, he sure was dedicated to killing deer.

I have said a lot about my father and the deer that he killed. I could talk all day about just the ones I know about. I spent a lot of my young life looking for deer that my father shot. You don't get an immediate kill every time, you know. I have followed deer for many miles. I have seen deer that were shot in the heart go a lot farther than you might expect and some of the gut shot ones would go for a mile or more. Every time they would jump and run, a piece of their innards would drop down and they would step on it and pull more out. Hunting is not always a clean kill.

You might think that he enjoyed killing. I never got that thought. But deer was not the only species of animal that he killed. He also killed birds, raccoons, and a lot of porcupines (we killed them for the bounty.) You did not need a gun for the porcupines. You could always catch them as they were not very fast. A club to the nose would usually get them. The state paid 50 cents per animal. What we needed was four paws, and we had to take them to the Surry store, Kendall Allen's store. Remember the nickname thing? He was called "Little Giant." He was short but built very well. He was authorized to pay out the bounty and give us our money. Kendall did not want to handle them. They were nasty. We would tell him we had so many and count them out to him and he would tell me to put them in the trash barrel that he burned periodically. Well, do you think we put them all in the barrel? I guess not! We put three paws per animal in the barrel and had some to take back home for a good start on our next batch.

Back to my father – all the time I was with him or heard his stories, I never got the feeling he was high on killing. We just did it. That was it.

My father had two guns. The first one I remember was a .30-40 Krag. At the time, it was a cheap gun. I think it was a military issue and had been cut down to be a deer rifle. Anyway, for years he used it and I would guess he killed 50 or more deer with it. Considering that many hunters only kill one a year if they are very fortunate, that is a lot!

One year he bought a brand new Winchester .30-30. It was just called the ".30," whereas the .30-40 Krag was called the "Krag." He did have an old single barrel shot gun and he did shoot deer with it, but mostly he used the Krag or the .30. When he got the .30, he decided that he wanted to be sure to keep the count of how many deer he shot with it. So every time he shot one, he put a little V notch with a file or his knife. He was careful doing it. By the time I left home, he had 73 notches on the .30. He tried a lot of tricks with that gun. He was always doing something like mounting special brackets to affix flashlights to the barrel or painting the front sight in order to see better at night. He shot a lot of deer. Just think about it. Some people reading this will doubt the claim, but trust me; I was at home for most of those years and personally involved with many of those kills.

(After my father died, that gun got sold to someone. Years later, I thought of that .30 and felt I would like to own it for old memory's sake. The owner told me when he first got it, he tried it out and it would not hit anything accurately. My father never cleaned his guns, so that was probably why. A lot of hunters clean their guns every time they shoot them.)

He fired right through the glass

What would you think about being waken up some morning by a rifle being fired right under your nose, almost literally? I was asleep one morning when I was awakened by my father firing his .30-40 Krag right below where I slept. Now, when I say right under, remember that I have been telling you about our low ceiling and just boards for a floor in the attic with cracks in it where I could look right down into the kitchen. What happened was that my father got up that morning and when he looked out the kitchen window, he saw a deer just a few feet from the house. He knew if he started outdoors, the deer would run away. So, without opening it, he fired right through the glass and shot the deer. This was before breakfast. He figured the glass didn't cost that much. We were a while without it being replaced though.

A lot of honey

I must have been eight or nine. My father was on one of his hunting jaunts up the Neck a couple of miles when he stumbled upon a giant tree that the wild bees must have been using for several years. There was lot of honey in it. Anyway, you can't just go cut these trees down. It's against the law, you know. Also, it was on someone else's land, and the tree was actually quite close to the road, only a few feet out of sight. We took the car and an old trailer and parked it out of the way so nobody would see what we were doing. (Seems like we were always hiding the car for some reason or another.)

We were a long time getting the tree down. Remember, it was before chain saws, at least way before we ever got one. So, with a buck saw and an axe, we got it down. Now, this thing weighs seven or eight hundred pounds. I could not even put my arms around it. We tugged and pried it so it was closer to the road, then we got the car and trailer and drove next to where it was. We had to time it so traffic did not come along while we were loading it. That sucker was heavy and I am sure I helped some, but eight or nine years old, and how much help was I, really? We had a small window of time to load, but we got it on and drove home and put it way up in the field about 300 feet from the house. We then cut about a two-foot section out of it and exposed the honey. Boy! You should have seen it! I never before or since have seen so much of it.

We probably ate off it for a couple of years. Many times we just had honey and hot biscuits for a meal. We just kept cutting chunks out of it and all us kids chewed on the wax just like gum – ate the honey comb and all.

Now I will tell you the other honey story. Down the Neck about eight miles was a summer person who kept bees, but he was gone a lot. My father had been hunting down around his house and knew about the bees kept there. He took the hive apart and took a couple of the layers of honey. He made it look like bears got into it, and it worked!

The man came home and found the honey and assumed that bears got it. He reported it to someone and the newspaper got a hold of it, printing a story about bears being in the area and taking the honey. Well, at our house, we had a great time with that story!

Frank and Annie

Annie Y. and her son, Bert (nicknamed Pid) were always nice and I remember Annie would pick us up in her car if we were walking. After we got in, she would say, "Look in the glove compartment and there might be some candy there." It was just a piece or two of hard candy, but it was some good to us. Annie worked for a summer professor from Harvard, an old bachelor. He was nice and had some money. Actually, he came to our wedding and brought a gift of several things that seemed strange at the time, but what a gift! It was a box filled with kitchen things that would come in handy, under-the-sink stuff, cleaning supplies and such – items that were not real expensive on their own, but a lot of it. 54 years and I still remember.

Bert went off to the army or something. I did not know him too much until he got out and was in the Guard. He did not marry until he was older and I am sure he was the main supporter of his mother, Annie. I don't know what happened to her husband. Maybe she didn't ever have one. Bert came from somewhere, and at that time I thought you had to get married to have kids. She sure did like the fire chief, though.

I want to tell you about Frank and Annie. If I were to guess her age at the time, I would say maybe 40-ish. Frank had grown-up children. Maybe he was 50 at the time. Frank got to be fire chief and I guess that gave him some status. It seemed like it at the time, though I was impressed by about anything at that point in my life. I was in the 6th grade. Seeing that Frank was the chief, he thought that he should have a place set aside in the old fire house, off to one corner, for a bed and a little spot to get some rest between fires or something. If they had a couple of fires a year, I would be surprised. He only lived a mile from the fire house.

I was a little naïve, but the older boys were not stupid. When they saw Frank's truck and Annie's car parked for long periods of time at the fire house, they knew what must be going on. So, boys being boys, they would routinely sneak up to the outside wall and listen to what was going on. With what they could hear, and what they could imagine, every time they saw Frank, they would say, "Frank, oh Frank!" Frank hated them for it, but what could he do. They kept it up for a long time.

Annie was not a skinny woman, I remember that. My father made jokes about her; said she was warm in the winter and shade in the summer. Poor old Annie. Somebody for everyone.

Something special

Most Christmases were not too full in the way of presents, though one Christmas must have been an especially good year financially, because we were told we could have anything we wanted that cost less than two dollars. (That was enough, because that was a lot of money.) It had to come out of the Sears Roebuck catalog. That catalog was the only way we had to know what might be out there.

Here is the sad part. We had a couple of weeks to make up our minds, and for the life of me, I could not see anything I wanted. If you have practically nothing, then you really don't want for anything. Not like today. Kids would have a lot of things to pick out. I finally decided on a hunting knife with a leather holder.

We always had a stocking to hang. Always. There would be an orange in the toe, and some candy, and then some sort of small present. I remember one Christmas my uncle bought me a small pen light, probably three inches long, so my parents put that in my stocking for a present. We were allowed to get up as early as we wanted, to get the stocking and take it back to bed with us. I don't know what time I got up, but it was early. Consider, no electricity, so no lights. I unwrapped my present but was not able to tell what it was. I fiddled with it and tried to guess. Even when daylight came, I could not figure out how it worked. I had never seen a penlight before and did not know something like that existed.

Easter was something special also. My mother would buy the green stuff that looked like shredded paper and it would line the birch bark baskets my father always made. He would go out in the woods and strip birch bark, and with one piece, fold it around to make a basket and a handle. I think he sewed it with thread. Anyway, it looked quite good and we had candy – probably chocolate Easter bunnies and other junk candies. May Day was done with the same type of baskets.

The Fourth of July was a time when we did things as a family. It usually meant a car ride somewhere. One year we went to visit my grandmother, Amanda. She lived in Somesville, on Mount Desert Island. I've told you about the poor cars we had. This one was not inspected and we needed an inspection sticker. During that time, the sticker had a different shape each year so an officer could tell by the shape if a car was inspected or not. My father cut just the right shape out of an old Christmas card so it would not be noticed by the police.

Another time, my Uncle Wesley and Aunt Dottie came down to spend the Fourth and do something with us. It was decided to go down to Bar Harbor and have a picnic. Big joke. We drove down to several places and each one was either too many people, not good enough, too much wind, too sunny – who knows why? We stopped at a lot of places and we kids hadn't eaten and it was in the middle of the afternoon. We finally ended up back on the mainland in Mariaville, on the River Road in a gravel pit. Some Fourth of July.

My mother could push my buttons

I actually took a swing at my mother once. Boy, I am glad I missed. My father saw me do it, and he knew why, but he jumped right in and stopped me from doing it again, though I wasn't going to. Boy, my mother could push my buttons.

Although she nagged and swore at me almost constantly, this one morning she had been on me for a while and I went into the other room with a pan of dried beans to pick over. Beans did not come all clean in those days. You always had to pick them over before cooking. Anyway, I sort of tried to get out of her way and she came in and kept right onto me. She was calling me a ---- ---- , one of her usual daily rants, and a stupid lazy b------. I don't know why, I just couldn't hold it in. My father was right there. He had been listening, but I guess it was giving him a rest from her. There I was, sitting on a chair with another chair in front of me with the pan of beans I was picking over. She had been at it long enough, so I jumped up and took a swing. I felt pretty stupid. I was surprised that she did not do anything about it. I was ten or so. Just like my bad rank cards. It was an all-summer, every day thing, reminding me how stupid I was. Kinda gets to you sometimes.

Surry Constable

About the time I was 12 or 13, my father became constable of the town of Surry. I think it began when Edgar "Puggy" Ingles was constable and needed help with the grange hall dances. The fire department in Surry put on the dances for many years and they needed someone there for safety. I believe that was how it came about. Soon after, my father ran for constable and got voted in for that job for the next 30 years. It was not a job for the faint-hearted. You have to be a little bit of a bastard to do the job and not be bothered that you have half of the town hating you. Anyway, my father really liked the prestige of doing it. It gave him a reason for carrying a gun and to mingle with the sheriff's department and sometimes with the state police. He would have his dates in court and he sure liked to stop people speeding going through HIS TOWN. He hated the bicyclists who pedaled through Surry every year. It was fashionable to pedal across the country and they would be stretched out for miles. I suppose they met up at the end of the day. They did no harm, but my father would stop and hassle them, looking for something wrong.

He was responsible for collecting dog tax from the natives in town. Everyone was required to license their animals and when they did not, the town clerk would sic my father on them. He would go to their homes and ask for the tax and they would often say they would go into the clerk's office and pay next week. Well, after a week or so, he would be back at their home to get onto them again. He loved it. There would be a summons and a court date. If it got right down to it, he could take their dog and have it "dispatched," which meant he took the dog on a rope, put it into his truck, pulling it close to the passenger side so the dog could not reach the driver. He would shoot the dog and usually dump it over the bridge on the Cross Road so it would go out with the tide. He kept any leash they might have had on. He had quite a collection of dog leashes. If you were low man on the totem pole in his book, he would harass the living hell out of you. He treated some people very badly. I don't know why. He was always dirt poor and he picked on those who had no more than he did. I knew what all the Surry people thought of him. It was quite obvious. He would go on the clam flats and see if everyone had a clamming license and arrest them if they did not, but he dug clams year round and hunted year round, in or out of season.

One time he was called about someone clamming on the mud flats down the Neck so we went on down. We saw their car. It was someone he knew, and he really wanted to get them in trouble, so we walked down to where they were clamming and my father asked to see their license. They had one, so he had to walk away. He was mad, but I was embarrassed. After all, they were only getting something to eat. As he walked back past their car, he was tempted to ruin it so they could not drive it. He didn't dare to, though, because they would have known who did it.

He actually stopped Linda, who is now a good friend of ours, for speeding. I found her name in his book. She was single, so her name was Thompson then. He kept very accurate journals of all his work for the town.

He took the Surry dances very seriously. He ran them with an iron hand. Boy, people hated him! No one said too much to me about him, but my friends thought he was miserable. During intermission he would go out to the car to drink with some of his friends. One time he was sitting in his pickup truck drinking with a buddy when a couple of men opened the door, dragged him out and kicked the living daylights out of him.

You should have seen him the next morning – banged up all over with bruises all over his body. He never knew who did it, but he had a pretty good idea it was some of the Kane family because he had had trouble with them. One Saturday night at the dance hall, one of them turned the lights off, and after he told them twice to leave them alone, they got into a fight. One was punching my father and I started getting into it and a woman got on my back and started ripping and scratching me. Somebody started on her and was pounding her and I noticed a man against the wall with a choke hold on my father. I got down on one knee and punched the guy a couple of times in the face but he would not let go of my father. I stood up, and with my dress shoes on, kicked him a couple of times in the face. He let go then, but later told me they were going to kill me. I had to be very careful for quite a while. I was sure they would do it. One of the Kane boys was in prison for a year for trying to kill someone with a broken bottle, so they were capable of it. Three of them were arrested and went to jail that night. So there was no doubt that when my father got beat that time, it was the Kane's, paying him back. I must have been staying at home about that time, because I remember walking through Ellsworth and at least a couple of miles out on the Surry Road every day after school. I was ready to run into the woods if someone stopped that I did not know. After a few weeks, I figured they were all mouth and I was able to relax a little.

My father harassed the kids in town who were getting into trouble a lot and one of them was his nephew, David Finch, the one he called "The Fink." He was always trying to get something on "The Fink." Well, one night "The Fink" and some of his friends snuck into his yard and stole the police revolver right out of his truck. They couldn't have gotten that close if he had a dog, but he hated dogs. The truck was less than 25 feet from the kitchen window and he was sitting right there where they could see him. Boy, he was a long time getting over that. He never found the gun even though he knew who took it.

Over the years, he would have deputies who worked under him. He always referred to them as deputy dogs. They did not like him either. They did, however, like the distinction of being in the Surry police force. After all, they had a badge and could carry a gun. They had a small measure of status and my father called the shots. Good set-up, huh?

When I was 14, I had been driving for a while, mostly down the Neck, but sometimes into Surry village. I was still a year too young for a driver's license. I was actually dropping my father off in Surry Village so he could get a ride to work with someone. I was heading home and had to stop for traffic before making my turn. I had to wait there for quite a few cars coming down into the village from Blue Hill. Unfortunately, the last car behind all the others was the state trooper. His name was Wentworth Wessel. But remember the nickname thing? To our family, he was known as "Wimpy Wessel." He looked me all over and decided to stop me. I turned down the Neck road, hoping he was not going to follow. Nope. He turned around and I knew it was for me. No doubt. I hurried as fast as I could and turned into a drive way of someone we knew, hoping again that he would go by and not see me. Those guys are trained, though, so I got a ticket and had to go to court and pay a fine – at 14 years of age! My father would not go with me. He did not want anyone to associate me with him. You see, he was just working up in the judicial system and he thought I might spoil it for him in some way.

A year later when I took my driver's test, the instructor gave me hell for driving without a license. I couldn't understand why he would care about that. I never forgot it – a lesson that you carry your past with you.

Cap'n McCormack

Cap'n McCormack and his wife did not live on the Neck but were friends of my father and mother. I don't know Mr. McCormack's first name. He was just Cap'n McCormack. My father said Cap'n never did work on a boat, and if he ever did, he was "captain of the head."

Cap'n lived on a side road in Surry and had a little farm. It was not much of a farm, but there was a garden and some livestock. I remember having to kill a bull of his. I must have been 12 or so – had to have been. He was going to be gone, and he told me how to do it. Tie the bull to a stake in the ground so he could not run and then hit the bull in the forehead with a large hammer. Well, I did it, but apparently was not hard enough and I had to hit him several times before I got him down. Then it was the old "cut the throat and gut him out" trick. No fun, but what you grow up with. I also learned to milk goats at his farm.

The Cap'n had an old Plymouth, I think a 1946, and that impressed me. I would often be with my father when they would talk, and something that really ticked me off was Cap'n would say, "Damn kids nowadays are lazy! Can't get any work out of any of them." It bothered me even at my young age, because he didn't seem to do anything, but I worked very hard at everything I did. His little farm was run by his wife. If you think about it, what do people say today about kids?? Lazy, right? Yet don't we know of many that really work hard?

Cap'n McCormack and his wife played cards with my father and mother every week. Sometimes they came to our house and sometimes my parents went to their place. The Cap'n always looked shipshape, so to speak. He was quite agile and he even had a trick where he would jump back and forth over a broomstick. I remember he liked to play footsies with any woman sitting at the table with him. His wife was the haggard one. She was from the Ozarks and looked the part. Imagine a small, skinny woman that had grown up poor and overworked. She was nice, but it sure was done the way the Cap'n wanted. My father said Cap'n McCormack was a gentleman farmer. He was the gentleman and his wife was the farmer. They moved away and I lost track of them after I got married.

1st, 2nd, and 3rd grade classes at the Surry
School. Robert is noted with an "R."

School Days

After we got up in the morning on school days, my mother would clear a spot on the table, rip off five pieces of waxed paper, lay the bread on them, and then spread a little deviled ham mixed with mustard. There would be at least one ashtray on the table and she would be making them with a cigarette hanging out of her mouth. I used to watch and try to pick the sandwich that did not get ashes on it.

We had peanut butter sometimes but it came in a can and it would settle. As hard as you tried you could never get the bottom stirred up real good, so when you got to the bottom, it was all hard. When the hens were laying, we could have egg salad.

There were times that I did not have a lunch. We just barely got up in time to meet the bus. My mother was never a morning person and most days we did not have time to get ready. We barely washed up and went months without brushing our teeth. We never had toothpaste. We dipped our tooth brush into a box of baking soda when we did brush. We did not just put some on it, but we actually dipped it into the same box that my mother would use for cooking. We never brushed our teeth on any regular basis.

If we got to school without something, we simply did not eat. There was nothing at school, only water from the cooler.

I remember one year we could not start school with the other kids. We had no clothes. I mean it. No shoes, sneakers, or anything for our feet, and no proper shirts or pants. Probably my mother did not order them soon enough. Every year we ordered our clothes from the Sears Roebuck catalog. We would leave cash in the mail box and the mail driver would get us a money order and the next day it would be sent along with the Sears order. Anyway, can you imagine how anyone would feel to be days late starting school and all the kids would know why.

I guess I was not a good student. I did not pass the first year of school but the teacher, Mrs. Bonsey, worked with me and I was able to get into second grade with my classmates so I did not really stay back. Mrs. Bonsey taught a long time in Surry. I was not too bad in English but math was my worst subject. I read a lot, and read every book in our little school library. We never had children's books at home, just stuff that my parents read, smut books and a lot of old detective magazines, full of pictures and stories for me to read. From our sleeping spot in the attic we could see and hear everything that went on with my mother and father. While playing cards and drinking in the kitchen, there were always the sexual conversations between them and all of their friends. As a young sprout, I learned a lot of bad stuff. All I had to do was lie on my mattress and look down at them, just four feet below. Boy, the stories I heard. I didn't understand them, but it was entertaining. When I was about 11 or 12, I had a girlfriend down the road. You know. Kid stuff. My father asked me (crudely) if I was having sex with her. I said, "No," and he said, "Why not?" I didn't answer. I was quite shy and got embarrassed easily.

I got to school by car. There was a man who had been hired by the town to pick us up and his name was Roger Kane. He was a relative, though I did not know it at the time.

I had been given money for the teacher one day and had a quarter to bring back home. I forgot and left it on my desk. I was dropped off by Roger and I went up to the house and my mother asked me for the money. When I said that I forgot it, she beat me and told me to walk back to the school and get it and don't come home until I had it. Man, I wasn't that old. Anyway, I was hurting quite a lot and still crying and walking to Surry when Roger came up the road from delivering the other kids down the Neck. He stopped and could see me walking and crying. He took me to the school and got my money for me and brought me back home.

The worst time was when my rank cards came out. At the end of the school year if the grades were not good enough, I would get a whipping and then all summer I would be reminded what a stupid bastard I was. It was a long summer, and boy, I always dreaded bringing that card home. As I got a little older, I was able to alter the card some and change it back when school started again. We had to save the rank card and bring it back when school started in the fall. Seems strange now that I have said it, and I don't think they do that anymore.

A lot of boys in my school were joining the boy scouts. I did not ever ask for much, but I did think that would be neat! Anyway, my father found out that Ned S., who led the boy scouts, was gay, only it was not gay then. If someone said you were gay, it simply meant you were in a happy mood. My father called him a fag, a queer, a homo. I did not know what queer was, but sometimes we would drive by where Mr. S. lived and I wondered what he looked like and how he would be different. We did not do much of anything that took us off the Neck road. I never did join the boy scouts.

Nobody plays marbles anymore, but it was the game to play from the time I started school up into the 5th grade. Using the heal of our shoe, we would make a shallow pot or hole in the ground, then smooth it all around. Then we would each roll a marble and whoever got closest to the hole would go first. When Colby and Adelbert Buzzell teamed up, you could not win! At the end of the session I would end up losing all my marbles and it would be a long time before I would get more. When Colby and Adelbert got home, they would share the winnings.

In the 5th grade, my classmate, Earle Stover, had a talking crow which was able to say quite a few words. Earle had tamed him somehow and that crow would fly from his house into the school and take things from the desk and other places. Finally he had to make him stay home. It was pretty neat.

We had a brook behind the old school and during recess we would go to the brook and up and down the sides. In the spring it was best, because it would flood and come up into the school yard. Nobody seemed to care and there was no fencing around the school yard. We had a wood shed behind the school and the older boys had to lug wood for the fire. It was a two-story building, so there were wood fires upstairs and down. The stoves were big boxes and before the new thermostatic models, it was always cold. When it was really cold the teacher would let us all huddle closer to the heat. The boy's and girl's bathrooms were down at the end of two long corridors, the length of the building. Just outside toilets, very cold. Again, there was no running water and not much heat. The water dispenser in school was the old glass bottle type.

In the 6th grade we moved to a new school and started having hot lunch. Boy, there was not a thing I didn't like, and we could have seconds and sometimes more. It was the nicest thing. We hardly ever had anything decent at home. Behind the school we had a frog pond and we boys made life miserable for the enormous bull frogs that were there. Again, we could go out in the woods and off the school grounds. I think there were only six of us in the 6th grade.

Our school was small, and when I was in the 7th grade I think there were only seven kids. In the 8th grade, there was only one. The 7th graders marched with her at graduation so she was not alone.

We always had hand-me-downs. I sure hated that. The stuff came from other kid's families that I went to school with. Some would say, "Oh, that looks good on you. I liked it when I used to wear it," or something like that. I hated it and will never forget how I used to feel. I'll repeat it. I hated it. I would not mind so much now, because I can buy it myself if I wanted to, but then we had no choice.

You know, for many years I had a problem with my left knee unlocking and dumping me on my face without any warning. With my stuttering so bad, I did not need that. Embarrassing! I would be running or walking along and it would dump me on my face. My knee did not hurt when I did it, and I would get right up, but it hurt when you went down face first, because it happened with no warning at all. It lasted years. I never went to a doctor with it. We never went to one except for large cuts that my father could not put together with what he referred to as "butterfly stitches."

I stayed at my Uncle Wesley's house on North Street once; I think just that one night. The next day I was out playing in the yard when someone was walking past and I hollered out, "Hi!" and he answered back, "Hi!" I then said to him, "Where are you going?" My Uncle Wesley heard me and asked me if I knew him, knowing full well that I did not. When I said no, he gave me a tongue-lashing that I still remember. He made it quite clear that it was the man's business where he was going and not mine. Funny how those things stick by you. I could not have been more than eight or nine years old.

In the same boat

My cousin Jimmy, probably a year younger than I am, came to visit me a couple of years ago with Timmy Taylor, a friend I have had since we were teenagers. Jimmy's father was "Junior" Greenlaw, married to my mother's sister, Irene. I think Jimmy is brilliant, but most of the Greenlaw family had a problem with reading, and with that goes math and other subjects that have to fit in with reading.

He and his family visited our family when I was eight or nine years old. They came up from the Bayside Road in Ellsworth, which in those days, was a long way for them to come. When they tried to explain where they lived, I could not fathom how I would get there. I knew where the town of Ellsworth was, but beyond that was a never-been zone.

We did go to their house, once - just a camp really, like ours. It was after a storm and a tree had come down through their roof and you could see it all opened up. A couple of weeks had passed and Junior had done nothing about it. It was a strange thing to see, and what helps me to remember is that my father made fun of Junior for hanging clothes on the limbs and chided him about not taking care of it. Man, if we were poor, they were in the same boat.

Irene left Junior and all her kids flat – just walked out. I can't imagine how Jimmy's life went after that. It wasn't good when she was there. Funny, it was not good enough for her to stay, but good enough for the kids.

Irene came to live with us for a while. When she was hungry, she would get food that I would have been slapped around for taking – or even asking for. A lot of people lived with us at different times, including my mother's sister, Thelma. She was always leaving her husband with the kids. My grandfather, Ed Mack, stayed several times, and so did my mother's brother, Freddy, when he was young, and my father's brother, Big Red.

Robert, 8th Grade

I had not mastered the art of stopping

When I was eleven or twelve, my father was off somewhere, maybe out cutting wood behind the house. His car, a 1936 Plymouth, was in the yard, and I sat in it and after a while I started it up. I got used to the clutch (this was before automatic cars) and I backed it up a few feet and ahead a few feet many times. I finally backed it up and got it headed down the driveway and I could not figure out how to stop it and back up, so I decided to let it coast down the driveway, get it turned around, and back up to the house.

Well, anyway, things did not get better after that. Now I was at the end of the driveway and I could not get it turned around. I thought if I went down the Neck a ways, I could find a place I could turn around without trouble. Well, I ended up going about two miles, and about one-half mile before the Carrying Place (where we had picnics) there was a car coming toward me. I was going slowly and it should not have been a problem, but remember, I had not yet mastered the art of stopping. As the car got closer and closer to me, the road did not seem to me to be wide enough for both cars, so I kept moving over closer to the ditch. By the time the car got real close to me, I was already in the ditch and slowly coming to a stop. I did not hit anything, but the car stalled out and I just sat there not knowing what to do. I knew I was in deep crap. It did not get any better after that.

The woman, Mrs. Delafield, who had the only car that came off that Neck road on a regular basis, stopped and asked if I was ok. I tried to start the car but it would not start, and I probably couldn't have gotten it out of the ditch anyway. She went on down the road and brought back a man with an old farm tractor to pull me out. Oh, man, it was slow, very slow. He had to tow me all the way up the Neck road to my house.

When we got close enough to see the house, it was a long time going slowly, so that I could see my father standing in the yard and also my mother and my uncle Red. I had a long time to think about how much trouble I was in. As you can imagine, it was not a good day for me. Did I learn something? Yeah, probably.

A room of my own and a real bed

In the fall of my 8th grade class, I was sent to live with an old lady named Lillian (Kane) Collins, and I stayed all winter until 8th grade graduation. She lived alone in a house that is no longer there, right on the main road leading out to Newberry Neck. My grandmother, Amanda, had been living with her and left to go cook for the wealthy summer folks in Bar Harbor. Lillian did not need any physical help, just someone to stay with her in case of trouble. I got no money or compensation of any kind, but Lillian did cook for me, so I actually ate quite well. "Three hots and a cot," they would call it. She did not drive and had no car, so we didn't ever go anywhere. I went to school every day, so I got out for that. Weekends, holidays, or any other time off from school were right there with Lillian. That was the first time I ever left my family. Thinking back, it was a long time to be away from them. They were just down the road two miles and they had to go by her house most every day, but my father came to visit only once, and I never saw my brothers or Sandy or my mother that whole winter.

The thing I remember quite well is that I had a room of my own and a real bed for the first time in my life. Lillian kept it changed and clean. There was no electricity, so it was just a room to sleep in, but it sure was nice. I did not miss being away from home.

Lillian got sick for a couple of weeks and I guess it was the flu or something. Her remedy was to get salt water mixed up and then she would sit in the kitchen with a wooden bucket between her legs. She would suck salt water up a nostril of her nose and pull it into her nasal passage. She would cough up phlegm and crap and spit it into the bucket. She would do this in the kitchen right next to the table while I was eating. That was bad enough, but one night she had cooked pea soup and Johnny cake for my supper. Getting that down with her spitting out phlegm was one thing, but she tipped over the wooden bucket and spilled the whole mess on the floor by my feet. I kept what was in me down. She was so sick, and I knew I should have helped her. She looked at me and said, "I guess I can't ask you to help me clean this up." I did not help her. I should have, and I still think about it.

When I moved out after graduation of 8th grade, she told me over and over again, "Don't forsake me now. Don't forsake me." I think she truly liked me and wanted me to keep in touch, but I never did see her again.

Robert, sitting in foreground, with his 8th grade graduating class at the Surry School. 1954

A terrible summer

The week after eighth grade graduation, I went to work for Paul C. who delivered milk and cheese and other dairy products from door to door for Morrison Dairy. Typically in the summer months they hired someone like me to help out on the home deliveries. I lived in Ellsworth with Paul and his wife Helen, and I think they had one son at the time. We started way before daylight and worked way after dark every day six days a week. We used an old milk truck with metal floors, an old Divco truck that was common for deliveries like that. That was a terrible summer. We covered most of the Down East area and Mount Desert Island. I would carry a metal rack with glass bottles in each hand and sometimes deliver to six or seven cottages at one time. It was hard work. I remember after my first couple of days on the job, I was told I could have anything I wanted on the milk truck. I had tasted cream before but it was something us kids were never allowed to have. Boy, I thought that would be good. That morning I drank two whole pints of cream. I was sicker than a dog, but I had to keep working all that day.

I was 14 years old and so tired all of the time that between stops I would lay down on the floor of the truck and fall asleep. On the trip to and from Bar Harbor, Paul would let me drop off to sleep but then would slam his hand down hard on my leg and it would hurt bad, quite bad. So, I could never get caught up on my rest. He was a slime ball. He would pick up men on our route and then drive off to some side road where they would perform sexual favors. He may have paid them a few dollars. I don't know. The chef of a restaurant where we regularly ate was gay and Paul was always trying to hook me up with him. He never was successful. I was shy and embarrassed and didn't know what to say. He got me drunk one night on *Miller High Life*, the "champagne of beer." He would show me his war photos – pictures of dead men and his warped buddies doing sexual stuff. He had a captive audience and I was it. These were pictures he kept away from his wife Helen. I was treated quite badly and I was always intimidated by him. My father and mother came to visit once and stayed only a few minutes with Paul and Helen and me. There was no way I could talk to them alone. I was trapped and could not do anything about it.

I had headaches all of my freshman year and I think it was because of the way I worked all summer on that milk delivery job getting just a few hours of sleep each day.

During the time of being with Lillian and working at the dairy, I only saw my parents a couple of times. Remember, there were no phones, and I would have no idea how to get in touch with them. The way I was treated working for the dairy was criminal and morally horrible. I should have been pulled out of there. I did earn ten dollars a week and saved every penny. I had eighty dollars in the bank when school began that fall which was enough to buy a winter coat and some Christmas presents for everyone in my family.

Only home for a couple of weeks

There were no school buses from Surry to Ellsworth High School, so I walked or rode a bike to Surry Village and started walking and hitchhiking to school every morning. After school it was worse because I had to walk from the high school through the town of Ellsworth and onto the Surry road far enough so someone would pick me up. I can remember times when I did not have any boots and I would pull old stockings up over my shoes.

I was only home in Surry for a few weeks until I moved in with my Uncle Fudd and Aunt Betty on North Street in Ellsworth. One time Fudd beat my cousin Philip with a wooden slab, a four-foot piece. He beat him badly, and all because he told Philip to lug wood in and I did it instead. Fudd figured it out somehow. He treated Betty's kids terribly and his own kids with her, ok. Philip and I have talked about that in the last few years. I got treated badly many times at home but not like that.

Anyway, I babysat for Aunt Betty, did dishes, milked the cow, and tended out in any way I could to pay my board. I had to go to bed one night at 8:30 and the other at 9:00. No excuses. She was very strict about that. During that time period, I would literally run the three miles to their house every day to eat lunch, and then run back to school. They would not give me hot lunch money (and shouldn't have.) I didn't think anything about it. Even a bottle of school milk was three or four cents and I just didn't have it.

I discovered something about my Uncle Fudd when I worked with him on a mail truck that winter at Christmastime. Fudd, whose real name was Evans H., was very crooked. He routinely stole from the mail truck. The mail came in sacks mostly, but boxes would be sent also. When the trains came into Ellsworth from Bangor we would off-load from wagons[2]

---

[2] These were 4-wheeled wagons with handles that could also be hooked to small motorized tractors that could pull one of them or a few, if necessary. The wheels had spokes with metal rims, not unlike a farm wagon, and the wheels were two feet high or more.

and when anything got accidentally put on a wagon heading down east, Fudd would put it on our truck and it would go home with him. He actually worked for E.D. Holt, the company that held the contract to run mail from Bangor to Ellsworth. Holt had several filling stations and a warehouse with supplies where the mail trucks were kept. We were the recipient of many things – a chainsaw once, tires, batteries, and motor oil, which he often sold to people that he knew at the train station. Someone was always coming up to him and saying, "Hey, Evans, here is some money I owe you."

During the day, I went to high school, but we would go to Bangor early in the evening and stay at a hotel called The Hancock House. Boy, was that place a dive, but think of the education I got there. Cockroaches were everywhere. You could actually hear them in the dark, and if you put the light on, you would see a lot of them before they would scurry out of the way. The doors of all the rooms were patched up with pieces of plywood. There was always a lot of noise and a lot of fights and things going on that I can only imagine. They had beds in every room that would vibrate when you put a dime in the machine. At the time I could not envision anything so modern. Pretty fancy, I thought. We would have to be at the train station around 3:00 AM, so we did not have much sleep anyway. We would have to wait for each train to come in (one from Northern Maine, one from Boston, etc., you get the picture) and there would be at least an hour before we could get all the trains loaded for Ellsworth. We would be in Ellsworth by around 7:00 or 7:30, then we would off-load to trucks heading to other parts of the state down east. Later in the day, those same trucks from Calais, Bar Harbor, Hancock, and other places, would bring back the mail from those areas and we would be off to Bangor again to catch those trains going out.

Around noontime, between mail runs, Fudd would watch "Queen for a Day." It was a TV show about a single woman or mother who was going through a difficult time in her life. They would feature her and make her queen for a day. When they would explain what terrible things she had been or was currently going through, Fudd would watch with tears running down his cheeks, feeling so bad for those women.

Fudd and Betty went out of town one week and I was in charge. I milked the cow in the morning before school and when I got home in the afternoon the barn was burning and the cow and the other animals were inside and could not get out. The cow was distressed a long time before it burned to death. I won't forget that. They figured out that oil was delivered that day and the delivery man must have been smoking. The house, only a few feet away, was destroyed too.

Robert, age 17, at Brookside
Restaurant, Ellsworth, Maine

I didn't seem to fit in

So, after the fire, I was out of a place to stay. That is how I made it to your Aunt Alice Berry. She had three or four boarders and needed help doing dishes and other household chores. I had to lug water from the well every night. I was getting quite used to living with people and doing things their way. Alice was a Pentecostal minister and she never got me to go to a meeting, but she would pray for me every Sunday afternoon before they went to their church meeting. It was loud enough for me to hear in the kitchen where I was earning my keep doing dishes. Alice only had a couple of dish wipers and they were very thin and cheap. They were always wet and I could do nothing about it. This work was only for my room and board and I had to share a bed with her son, Jackson. He was about 12 years old but he was very heavy and his weight in the old bed made it sag to his side. I had to sleep hanging onto the rail under the bed; otherwise I would just go to the middle. It was a small bed, not even a full size, which would have helped.

I still had no money to call my own, so eventually I got a job up the road for Mr. and Mrs. Alvarado. He was a machinist and worked every day in Ellsworth. They had a farm, and they were always behind in the farm work. Most of the animals were more like pets. One pig was hundreds of pounds, too old and fat to be any good for market. Saturday and Sunday I worked all day, long days. I got paid six dollars for the two days' work and it paid for my hot lunch every week. That was a concern for me, having something to eat at noontime. I can remember when I was staying at home and had no money, I would leave the school house and walk off the school grounds until I thought the hot lunch was over and then come back. Man, it sure smelled good when I got back.

I did go home for a while, but I think that was in my third year of high school. I don't know how long, maybe weeks, but I had been gone a long time and I didn't seem to fit in. Just my thinking, I guess. Walter and Sandra grew up a little while I was gone, so I missed a few years. Through high school, I would go home from time to time but the dates are fuzzy.

In my sophomore year I got a job with a restaurant washing dishes. I was paid ten dollars for an eight-hour shift. I worked two shifts all summer because it gave me more money. It was the largest restaurant in Ellsworth; Brookside, and it had its own bakery and chef, even a potato peeler. It was really quite nice. Brookside is gone now. It burned down. With the insurance money, Frank A. built a new restaurant, Jasper T. started his own place, and Buster G., stayed in the construction trade. Everyone made out except the insurance company.

In my senior year I lived with Aunt Ruth and Uncle Chippy, also in Ellsworth. Apparently there were some sort of hard feelings between my father and his sister, Ruth, because he went years without speaking to her and I saw my parents very, very little during the time I stayed with her.

He thanked me for stopping

I had been driving my car without a spare for days and needed one badly. I must have been at least 16 at the time. Coming to Surry from Ellsworth one night, late, after 12:00, I saw a car parked alongside the road without lights.

I could see that car had the same wheels and tires I needed, so after I glanced quickly into the car and saw that it was empty, I opened the trunk to take the spare. No spare. I slammed down the trunk lid and opened up the passenger side rear door (it was the custom in those days to just roll the extra tire into the back seat.) No spare there, either. Since I wasn't getting a spare tire, I decided to check if there was anything in the front seat or glove compartment that I wanted.

I opened the passenger front door and this man flopped out! I asked him if he was ok. He thanked me for stopping and I drove out of there before his head could clear up.

Tony Moon and Robert Stevens. 1956

I nearly drowned there

One summer day, my friend Tony Moon, and I took a trip down to the quarry in Sullivan. Those quarries were worked for nearly a hundred years, and although some in Maine are still in operation, most were out around 1900. They operated below the water level so after they stopped working and stopped pumping out water, they very quickly filled up. This quarry was easy to get to and was used by young people from all over. I know for a fact that several people drowned at that quarry and I know of one vehicle that ended up on the bottom. I know this because I nearly drowned there myself. Here's why: Remember I told you that until I left home, I only swam in salt water. I would dive head first off the rocks around the shore, but nothing very high. Well, salt water has a lot of buoyancy, a lot more than fresh water. Boy, at that quarry, I dove head first off a ledge that was at least 15 feet high and I went down and went down – a lot more than I had ever been. I ran out of air and just made it up before I had to breathe. It was scary. I had heard about that quarry for a long time and couldn't wait to get there. I went down there on my motorcycle a few years ago just to see it again and it sure didn't hold the appeal that it did when I was young.

Well, Tony and I swam there for a while, and then we went to another quarry close by that was still operating. We went in and looked around and saw an old donkey engine. This was just a motor that ran the boom to move granite from one place to another and loaded up stone for shipment. Well, junk metal was something always on my mind, so Tony and I took the radiator off of the engine. We took it to Sargent's junk yard in Ellsworth and I think we got seven dollars for the radiator. I thought that was the end of it until my father came into the blueberry field one day, walked down to where I was raking, and said, "You been down to Sullivan lately?" I said, "Yeah, why, how did you know that?" He told me the sheriff was in the car with him and wanted to talk to me. The police had gone to Tony first and tried to get him to rat on me. He would not do it and took all the blame. When they came to me, I did the same thing, with one exception. They decided to let me take the blame. That was a test of friendship, taking the blame for someone else.

My father was upset and said I was stupid not to have handled it better so as not to get caught. The guy at the junk yard almost ended up going to prison. He was responsible for accepting stolen goods and he wasn't very happy about that. The police went to him first after the quarry reported the radiator was stolen. They were notorious for buying junk without asking questions. Where did they think two young boys got that radiator? Anyway, I knew it was not going to be pleasant returning the money to him. Boy, did he read me out!! I had it coming, though. Then I had to see the sheriff and show him the receipt that I got for returning the money.

When he was young

All the time I was growing up, my father told us stories about when he was young. In Massachusetts, his family lived in an apartment building. It is hard to believe that my father and his brothers would be a source of irritation to anyone, but one of the other tenants did not like kids, and he would kick at the toys left on or near the walkway each time he came and went. After a while, the Stevens' boys drove a metal stake in the ground, and the next time he kicked one of their toys, he hurt his foot. He never kicked their toys again.

They would repeatedly ring the neighbor's doorbell, and run away. The man was enraged. The boys had it figured out just right, and when they thought they had him at a certain point, they tied a string across the door step and then they all pooped on the step. When they rang the doorbell this time, he came rushing out to catch them and he fell into the poop.

The attendant at the local dump would grab anything you happened to lay aside while you were unloading your truck. That dump attendant was a miserable character, so for several days my father would poop into an old shoebox. He tied it up with a ribbon and set it right on the pile of rubbish. I guess that dump attendant must not have been too happy about that.

In the 1930's, work was almost non-existent and many people went across the country looking for anything they might find. My father rode the railroads. It was illegal to do so, and the railroad "bulls" carried guns and inspected the cars to see if anyone was on that should not be there. Many times they would scurry off because getting caught meant jail time.

Once, my father was running away and the railroad cop yelled for him to stop. He kept running, and the cop shot him twice in the lower leg. (He always had those two scars, on both sides of his leg.) When he told us this story, I asked him, "Did you stop, then?" and he said, "Hell, no. I ran even faster."

Another time when they were riding the train in California, they could see fires burning in the mountains. The train stopped right in the desert and they had no place to run, so they all had to get off the train and fight the fire. It was either that or be sent to jail. Forced into it, they fought the fire for days.

Robert's father, Russell K.Stevens,
in New York City, 1927.

While he was in California, he met a man in a bar who had a new pickup and wanted my father to help him get copper wire to sell as junk. He and my father drove out on the desert and climbed telephone poles with a hatchet and a block of wood. They would hold the block of wood and cut the wire from pole to pole, and after spending as much time as they dared, they drove farther into the desert and burned off the wire's insulation, then sold it to junk yards. They did that for quite a while and did quite well until my father found out the man had also stolen the pickup, so they parted ways. He figured the truck would eventually be tracked down.

While hitchhiking across the long desert, a car load of men stopped ahead of my father as if to pick him up. When he ran up to the car, they pulled ahead so he had to run again to catch up to them. When they did it a second time, my father picked up a large rock and flung it through the rear window. There was no tempered glass back then, so it would have been completely taken out. He was fast, and was able to get away from them safely.

He ended up in jail

When my father was in his early 20's, he was in a port in Cardiff, Wales, and as usual went to the nearest bar. Apparently he got into a fight and I think the other fellow was using a knife. Anyway, he ended up in jail for disorderly conduct. Not his first or last time in jail.

When he came up before the judge, he could not prove who he was, so the judge ordered him to send to Surry, Maine, to get a copy of his birth certificate. Well, he had to stay in jail until it came, (no faxes in those days,) and when it did come, it wasn't notarized. The judge probably decided that it cost more to keep him than to make arrangements for him to get out of their area. He was ordered to sign on to a tramp vessel that was hauling case oil into the US. His first stop was Port Arthur, Texas.

As soon as he got the chance, he jumped ship in Port Arthur, and started hitchhiking across the US to get to Maine. He told me he went three days without food. I am sure he did not have any money on him and he could not get any from the steamship line until he signed off on their final destination. He told me a truck driver bought a hamburger for him.

He never dared to sign on to another ship because they kept good records and probably would have found out he had gone to jail.

King of the hobos

My Uncle Irving Stevens' wife, Mary, left him with five children, so my mother babysat for his youngest for quite a while. That kid was treated very badly. He was only two or three at the time, and he got a lot of spankings and mistreatment. Irving showed up every Friday night without fail and paid my mother for doing it. Times were very hard for poor old Irving. All the kids went to different homes but eventually he got them all together again. They always respected their father.

My father always said that Irving was a dreamer. Perhaps I could agree with him some, but Irving was the only one of his brothers who did not always look for a fight or some sort of trouble. He saved his money and always sent some home to his mother. He was the one who loaned my father $200 for the land he bought (the other $200, he earned cutting wood on the property.) When I was a small child, I thought of Irving as different from the others. He played the harmonica, and he whittled airplanes with propellers out of wood, sticking them up in the big pine tree behind my grandmother's house. If the wind was blowing at all, I could hear the propellers turning. I thought it was pretty neat. I could not imagine how those airplanes got up there so high. How many people do you know who would do that?

When Irving was a young man, he rode the rails and saw a lot of the country, living life as a hobo. He was quiet and soft-spoken and everyone liked him. I told you he wrote some books. He wrote about his experiences. He published "Hoboing in the 1930's," "Mandy's Washtub and Other Stories," "National King of the Hobos: An Autobiography," and a couple of others. He peddled them all over the state, but not just the books. Here's what he did.

Every spring, he made up a batch of fly dope in his bath tub and bottled it. It was under his own label and was called "Irving's Fly Dope." He had a passel of what he called "anticdopes." (Yes, that is spelled right.) These were little slips of paper with his quips on them. He had a lot and I wish I could remember more of them. The only one that comes to my mind is, "All flies hate dopes, but especially Irving's."

He was elected "King of the Hobos" for several years at their annual week-long convention in Britt, Ohio. The group's official web site says, "Ask a veteran hobo what a hobo is and you'll receive a definite answer. The hobo is a migratory worker; some with a special skill or trade, others ready to work at any task, but always willing to work to make his way.

The tramp, they'll tell you, is a traveling non-worker, moving from town to town, but never willing to work for the handouts that he begs for. A bum is the lowest class; too lazy to roam around and never works.

Misunderstood and mistreated, the wandering hobos have come to find understanding and friendship in the town of Britt, Ohio."

When Irving got too old to travel to the convention by himself, his daughter, Connie, went with him and for several years she became "Queen of the Hobos." For those who don't know about the Britt gathering, it is quite a shindig. The town is filled with hobos, retired and active, supporters, and even a few well-known entertainers.

His book, "Dear Fishbones" was a 30-page publication of questions from a fourth-grade class in Sherman Mills, Maine. It came from a visit Irving made to their class in 1989 where he explained the symbols that hobos used to communicate with each other and the different situations that they ran into.

My father ran the railroads too, and he was with Irving during some of those times. They would hit a town and split it up between themselves, looking for small jobs that would get them something to eat. Irving would usually do better. My father said Irving was neater looking and had a more honest face. It was not a very good life, but times were tough during the depression. I heard them say, "You couldn't even buy a job." I suppose they didn't want to admit to begging, but I believe that is what they had to do sometimes.

Irving worked for a shoe factory for many years and retired from there. He was a State of Maine champion for playing horseshoes. He was good, so at our family reunions, guess what he brought to play for a game? Yeah, you guessed it. Horseshoes! What kind of chance did we have?

The black sheep of Surry for a while

When I got older, I thought nothing of having someone drive 100 miles an hour while I climbed out the front window and back into the car through the back door window. We would drive out the Bucksport Road in Ellsworth and play chicken with other drivers or drag race on that same road. We even had the road striped off for our quarter-mile run. The police couldn't catch us because we had such a long stretch to see them first. Boy, they sure tried. They used to follow me around town even though I was doing nothing wrong, waiting for me to slip up. The state police stopped me in Surry once and actually drove my car to see if they could find something wrong with it. That was illegal, but what could I say, and who would I say it to?

One summer during school break, I was headed home to Surry. I was working two shifts at the Brookside restaurant and was very late coming home. My father was always telling us kids about the things he did as a kid, stuff like taking apart a whole wagon and putting it together again on the roof of a store. Another time, he got hold of some dynamite and put several sticks of it on a slab of wood and pushed it out into Surry Bay. If you think about Surry Bay, it is just like a big amphitheater, and when that blasted off late at night, nobody slept. Some of those things were sort of going through my mind and I got to thinking, "What do I have to talk about when I get old?" As I went through Surry, it came to me.

I parked the car down the road about one quarter of a mile and walked back up to the Methodist church. By that time my eyes were adjusted to the darkness and I went into the church. The door was not locked, and I went around to the back where I knew the bell rope hung. Kinda dumb, I guess, but I went up the ladder that was nailed to the wall, taking the rope with me. Well, look, I had to go through a hole in the ceiling just like the one I climbed through every night at home. Anyway, I rang the bell until I just could not do it anymore. I was bushed. So, I rested a few minutes and started again. I was in good shape then, so I did it justice. When I rested the second time, I heard the door open. I knew then I was in deep doo doo. I went into the back of a wall that came straight up to make another room in the church. I don't know what I was thinking. Maybe they would go away and then I could get down and get out of there. Turns out, it was Joe Telford. Old Joe was a staunch Catholic and attended his church faithfully. He was a nice guy but his wife Edna left a little to be desired. Edna attended the Methodist church and she ran it. Joe did the janitor work. He was scared because he did not know who was up there. I kinda felt bad. He came up under the hole and hollered up, "Come on down! Come on down!" He started up the ladder and every couple of steps he would holler again, "Come on down! Come on down!"

I'll give old Joe credit. He kept coming up those steps until he had his head up through the trap door and he still could not see me, though he should have heard me. My heart was pounding and seemed like it would come right out of my chest. He finally got all the way up and slowly got over to where I was crouching and shined a flashlight on me. He spoke kindly to me, "OK, let's get down out of here." So we got down and that was when the fun started. Edna (and the whole town) was awake, and she came into the church to see who would do such a thing. She kept saying, "Well, let me tell you," and "All I got to say..." Poor old Joe. She blamed me, but Joe was the one who left the door open after she had told him to lock it, and she went on and on. I ran down to the car and got out of there. I slept good that night.

I was the black sheep of Surry for a while, but it wasn't too long before I got redeemed when I stole a lot of fireworks that were supposed to go to Bar Harbor for the Fourth. I set them off on the other side of Surry Bay, but not before I went to the store and told them what I was going to do. Pretty good show, and they did not have to go to Bar Harbor to see them!

Robert Russell Stevens, age 17, with
a 1941 Plymouth, his first car.

We had to be very clever

As long as I can remember, my father did not have a decent car to use. He most always had old Dodges or Plymouths that were worn out long before he got them. I told you about the old dug-out foundation (or cellar hole, as we called it) that was in front of our house. In order to start these cars, we would pump them and sometimes pour ether in the carburetor, and then we would let it roll down the cellar hole and jump it in second gear. In those days, you could buy ether at any drug store in one-pound cans. You can't do that anymore. What they have today is called starting fluid but it is not the same thing.

One time when he needed to go somewhere and could not get the car to start, we hooked the horse to the car and got it going that way. If we needed a part under the car, we simply turned the car up on its side. It was easy. So we always had at least a couple of cars in the yard or field on their side or their top. Any old cars never left the premises, just got towed around the house and used for storage.

We had an old tractor and saw rig, and when we needed gas to run them we just siphoned some out of the car tank. When we needed a funnel for this or any other type of liquid, we would make our own. Remember, there was no plastic then, just glass bottles. We would take a bottle and tie a string tightly where we wanted the bottle to break and dip the bottle in some gasoline. This would soak the string with gas. Then we would light the string and let it burn down. The string would heat the bottle. Then, quickly, we would dip the bottle in cold water. The bottom would snap right off. Then we would sand the edges or twist it in the sand or dirt a couple of times to take off the sharp edge. It was a different time and we had to be very clever about some things.

Robert, age 17, in his 1941 Plymouth.

There was always something to be worried about

Going to Ellsworth from Surry was only about 13 miles and certainly not a problem today, but back then not many folks had cars, and in the winter a lot of people put them away. Before the use of snow tires (I saw my first "snow tire" about 1953) everyone carried tire chains. The problem was, the links would break and bang up against the side of the fenders and as soon as you got out of a bad spot, you would want to take them off.

Any old-timers will remember that we only had alcohol for our radiators, and if you got into a bad spot and started spinning, the motor would heat up and boil out all of the alcohol in the radiator. Nowadays we have *Prestone* anti-freeze that we put in our radiators and it will not boil out, not matter how hot the engine gets. Alcohol kept the radiator from freezing, but it boiled at a low temperature and just disappeared from the radiator, so, no protection, just water left. If it was cold out, the motor had to be completely drained or it would freeze up and ruin the car. You could add alcohol and save it, but if no money, then no alcohol. It was a constant battle.

While we are on this subject, those cars only had a 6-volt battery and did not start as easily as today, so when it was cold weather we would drain the oil out every night and put it on the back of the stove. The next morning, we would put it back in. Sometimes we would build a fire in an old pan to heat up the bottom of the motor or use a blow torch to apply heat to the manifold. If the battery was up and ether was dumped into the carburetor and you held your tongue in your mouth just right, it might start. It just was a miserable way to start your day. Without electricity, we had no way to charge up a battery, so we had to jump start the car and get it running before it could be charged up. The old 6-volt cars had a small generator and it took forever to charge one up.

There was always something to be worried about: getting stuck and losing your radiator protection, knowing you had no money and thinking what had to be done when you got home, and the next morning, and maybe many mornings before you got back to having your car protected, bad batteries, bad starters, bad points, bad plugs, and a few other things.

All the old cars I bought and drove were a constant problem for me. I grew to be a fairly good mechanic and can do most anything (within reason) on vehicles, however; my father was never especially good at it and I sure did not learn from him. It was a painful learning curve.

To back up a bit, the first car I drove, legally, was an old 1938 Buick that I took my driver's test in. Then it was on to a 1941 Plymouth. That car had a habit, and a bad one I might say, of slipping the timing. Now what it actually did was slip the distributor shaft, and it always seemed to happen when I really needed to be somewhere in a hurry. No matter where it stopped, and it did not always pick a nice place to do that, right then I would have to take out the distributor and turn the shaft around 180 degrees and then it would go ok. I swear that car could not take any dampness and it would not start. I always said that if a dog peed on the wheels, it would not go. That was one problem. I rarely owned a car that was ready to pass inspection, so once a year there was the strain of trying to get it ready.

There was a place in Blue Hill that I would go for inspection. I never had brakes that worked like they should, and emergency brakes were out of the question. To get a sticker, I would stop about a half mile before the station and climb under the ass-end of the car and adjust the rear brakes up as hard as they would go. Then I would drive the car to the station. By the time I got there, the brakes were hot and I barely got the car into the yard. Out the inspector would come and pull the emergency brake and try to move the car. Couldn't move it, so I got the sticker. I would have to stand around long enough for the brakes to cool off so I could drive off far enough to get back under the old wreck and back off the brakes so I could drive it. Most of my cars were about the same thing. Same sort of problems. Tires were always bad, too, so I was changing them constantly.

Something funny I have to mention. It was probably around the middle to late 40's that we saw our first flathead V8 engine. It was an old Ford, and a neighbor had bought it and stopped to show it to my father. Everybody in those days would show off their new (second-hand) cars. It was common to lift up the hood and look in and just talk cars and everything else leaning over the hood.

Anyway, we were looking at the motor and the guy was explaining how well it started in the mornings. My father said, "Well, it should. If one side doesn't start, then the other side has to." That was a dumb thing to say, but what did we know? We had never seen a V8 engine and didn't know anything about them though they had been making them for many years.

I thought I had killed him

One time, I was in the car and ran over a deer. I thought I had killed him, so I dragged him into the back seat of the car. I must have just knocked him out, because after I had driven for a while, the deer came alive! Well, he could not get up because his legs were kind of bent around the seat, but he sure was trying, and making a lot of commotion! I drove the rest of the way home with the driver's door open (I expected to dive out at any time) and pulled into the yard.

I stood in the yard for a few minutes to get my wind and calm down. I went into the house and my father was sitting at the table. As calmly as I could, I asked him if he wanted a deer. "Yeah," he said, "Where is he?" He thought it was up the road somewhere and we would go shoot it. "Well," I said, "I got one in the car, but he is alive."

"You're -------- me!" he said. We walked out to the car and there was the deer, trying to get up. "I'll be a son of a -----! I guess you have," he said. He shut the door, went into the house, got his knife, went back to the car, opened the door and cut the deer's throat. A lot of blood got on the floor of the car, but that was a common way of living to me and I didn't think much about it at the time. Cars were built stronger then. I didn't know of anyone who damaged their car by hitting a deer. Nowadays a car can be totaled for hitting an animal.

Walter, Robert, Tommy, Wesley, Sandra, and Dorathy, with a 1938 Buick. c. 1955.

Baby of the family

Walter was the youngest and seemed to get away with a lot. He was always destroying cars and getting into fights. He drank a lot and had a very nasty disposition when he was drinking. My father and mother put up with a lot from him but it didn't seem to bother them.

At one point, Walter was driving a nice little 1949 Chevy. He was staying with your mother and me one weekend and when I got up in the morning I saw the entire side of his car was demolished. One door on the passenger side was completely off. He was not up yet, so I went down the road a bit and saw where he went off and hit a utility pole. He had not broken the pole, but everything he had in the car was strewn all along the ditch. Well, I went back home and there were a lot of police cars in my yard. Walter got up then, and talked to the police, but nothing worried him. He had totaled the car.

I owned and operated an auto body repair shop in Ellsworth for several years, and one morning Walter came into my shop to have me look at his car. He stood around for a while talking, you know, like nothing happened. Well, he had picked up one of the Mulhern boy's girlfriends, and after he dropped her off, the boyfriend found out about it. He caught up with Walter and shot at him several times with a 30-30. The bullets had put several holes in the trunk area and hit the chrome above the rear window. The rear window was gone completely. One bullet was spent, but got through the driver's seat. A couple of inches and it would have been in his back. Mulhern was driving at a great rate of speed to keep up with Walter and shooting out the driver's side window. I call that pretty good shooting. With all the trouble he got into, nobody would have been surprised if Walter had gotten killed by someone. He wasn't going to have the car fixed, but the police arrested Mulhern and they wanted an estimate for the damages. This had happened right in town Ellsworth, and the cops really frown on shooting a 30-30 rifle in their town, especially many times. I don't really think they cared if Walter got killed.

Some time had gone by. I put in a rear window to keep out the weather and kinda forgot about it until one day Mulhern came into the shop and said, "I've got some money for you." Well, it surprised me. I knew him pretty well and told him I figured that Walter was gonna get it someday, but I was surprised it had come from him. Then I told him I felt bad about taking his money. He had to have borrowed it or something. It came hard to him, I'm sure of that. He said, "No, no. Don't worry about it. I will do anything. If I don't pay you and get a receipt, they are going to throw me in jail. No, no. I don't mind paying you."

Walter never did have any more work done on his car. Probably wore it out within a couple of weeks. Boy! He was murder on a piece of equipment. Just a few weeks later, he came in the shop just to talk. Within minutes after he left, I heard sirens and later heard that he had turned his car over several times on the Surry Road. Broad daylight - Summertime. I know of several totaled vehicles that should have killed him.

In the end, it was the "Big C" that did him in. With all his antics, he had a lot of friends at his memorial service. We had always gotten along well and I liked him very much. He was an avid reader and could converse on just about any subject. Walter never did stop drinking and smoking until his death. I went to see him just before he died and told him I was sorry he had to die and he said, "Ahh, ---- happens. You live. You die." I never had a chance to speak to him again.

He told me he was going to kill me

One evening, your mother and I went to Cunningham's Market on High Street for a few groceries. We had you and John. You were small. I had to hold both of your hands and I took you two in the store with me while your mother stayed in the car. Maybe she had a baby with her. Don't remember.

I walked through the store and picked up what we needed and headed for the cash register. The cashier was just starting to ring me up when this big guy came up to the counter and stated he wanted a case of beer. The cashier looked at me and I said, "Go ahead," though it was my turn. So, I am standing at the cash register with you two and the big guy was there also. He said, "How are you doing?"

I could tell he was drinking and I had no reason to be impolite, so I just said, "Fine." He looked like he was "loaded for bear," but he did not bother me. He went out before me, and I thought I had seen the last of him. I was between two cars and about to get you and John in the driver's side door and into the car when he showed up in front of my car. I saw him and he said, "How are you doing?" and again I said, "Doing good." Then he pointed to your mother and said, "Not you. Her."

I practically shoved you kids into the car. Your mother was upset and asking me to go, but I had no intention of doing that. I met him right in front of my car. He said, "Don't get tough," and I gave him a push as hard as I could and HE DID NOT MOVE. I kinda knew right then I was in trouble, so I hit him a couple of times in the face and it did not seem to bother him at all. We were right against my driver's door and he was bent over some, with his big hands around my head trying to push my eyes out. I hit him at least 25 or 30 times and he finally let go. We worked our way behind the car and in the parking lot and started fist fighting. I could hit him several times but every time he hit me in the face, I would fall down – could not stay standing up. So, I would get right up and hit him a few more times. I wasn't losing, but did not seem to be gaining a lot either.

A crowd started to gather and they broke us up. He told me he was going to kill me, and I didn't say anything kind to him either. I found out he was quite capable of killing me, so I had to watch my step for a while.

Boy, he looked bad

My father had two major tractor accidents in his life, either of which could have killed him. The first one occurred about a half mile behind the house. You may have heard about a tree that is called a "widow-maker." That is a tree that got hung up (when it was cut) and did not come down the way it was supposed to. Well, most will stay away from it until it can be taken down safely. Not my Daddy. He backed up to the tree and hooked a chain to it and tried to pull it down. The tree started moving and then the base of the tree caught on another stump. The tree fell down on my father and pinned him into the tractor seat. It was an old spruce tree and it had a lot of small branches. Not only did it pin him, but it poked a lot of holes in him. Well, he knew he was in a bad spot and the tractor was running, so the only thing to do was put it in low gear and drive out from under it. He went all the way back to the house, unhooked the twitch of wood he had on it, and put the tractor away, knowing he would not be working for a long time. He drove himself to the hospital and did not work for weeks.

The second tractor accident happened many years later when he was working on the starter of the tractor, standing alongside it. The tractor started up in low gear and rolled over his whole right side. I mean the whole right side! It started at his lower leg and went up and broke several ribs and punctured his lungs and continued over his head, breaking his jaw and crushing his face so that he lost his right eye. This time we thought he was done. All five of us kids went to Ellsworth Hospital to say goodbye.

Boy, he looked bad, to say the least. He was alert though, and could talk a little. Not too bad, considering the crushed jaw. The tractor had what is called "Canadian chains," big rings with extra large chains attached. It would have been bad enough with just the tires, but those chains did a job on him. He had to be transported to a larger hospital in Bangor for care.

Before they sent him off from Ellsworth, my brother Tommy came up to the bed and said, "Hey Daddy, I got some bad news for you. You did not win the lottery." Every week Tommy would buy two $1 tickets and would go down to my father's and together they would watch the numbers as they were shown on television. I don't know how he could do it, but he laughed.

He was in the hospital for many weeks and all of us kids got together and made out his obituary. He slept a lot; many times he was not even aware we were there to see him. We left notes for each other in his room so we would know who had been there and when. Son of a gun! He eventually got better – enough to come back home, though he never did drive again after that. My father was always an accident waiting to happen and he had had his share of them.

I want to tell you about when he was admitted to the nursing home in Ellsworth. After weeks in Bangor Hospital, then rehab, he was brought by ambulance to the nursing home and I was there when they brought him in.

My father asked the young nurse that was admitting him, "How are you doing?" She said, "Fine." He asked her, "How is your father doing?" and she said, "Fine." He asked, "How is your mother?" and again she said, "OK." Finally he asked, "Who are you, anyway?"

Toward the end of his life, when he was living by himself, I would call him every day to see how he was doing. He would from time to time say he should just blow his head off and get it over with. (He tried to talk his younger brother, Little Red Stevens [Harold], into drowning himself off the dock in Surry Bay. Red just could not do it, and died with pancreatic cancer.) I finally got sick my father's threatening, so the next time he said he was going to blow his head off, I asked him to call me before he did it. He said, "You really want me to do that??" I said, "Yes. I want to come over and clean up the mess before Sandy gets here." From then on, he would say, "I would like to shoot myself, but that would not be fair to Sandra."

My mother never went to doctors. I don't know what killed her. She went to the hospital and was pronounced ok and was coming home the next day. She went into a coma and died within a few hours. My own thoughts were that denial of liquor and cigarettes was too hard on her system. My father, though, should have died many, many years earlier. The tractor accidents alone should have done him in. He had an enlarged heart and it finally caught up with him. For a couple of weeks he was in the hospital and would say, "I wish the hell I would have a heart attack and die." Well, of course, that is what happened.

The day he died, my sister and I went to visit him and to tell the doctor he did not want to be resuscitated if he croaked. He wanted it over. Well, we went to the nurse's station asking to see the doctor but he was busy and the nurse said, "Why don't you go see your father and I will send him down when he comes back."

Always, when I went to see my father, he was sleeping. I would tap his feet and ask him if he was going to sleep all day. Well, he had been out for hours, like in a coma, and they didn't think he would come to. Anyway, I tapped him on the feet like usual and damned if he didn't wake up. He was trying to talk and his mouth was dry. I gave him some water and wet his lips and he started talking – mostly just thanking Sandy and me for helping him. Can't tell you everything, you know.

Well, in came the doctor, and in a loud voice he began talking to my father. Daddy looked at me and laughed and said, "Look at the stupid -------! He thinks I am deaf. I might be dying, but I am not deaf!"

He died that night. I called Sandy around 11:30 PM and we went down to see him. Took his watch and gave it to my brother, Wesley. Thought he might like it. The next morning, Sandy and I were sitting with the funeral director and the man was talking in a low soft voice. You know how they talk, like they are going to wake someone up. My father had instructed us that he wanted to be cremated, so Sandy said to me, "What do you think they will do with the pacemaker?" The man perked up then and said, "He has a pacemaker?!" kinda excited like. He then caught himself and said, "Oh, we'll take it out." So I asked him, "Why, what would happen?" He explained that if it was not taken out, it would blow up.

Sandy and I began laughing and he must have wondered, they just lost their father and they think it is funny? We then explained that our father loved noise and dynamite and if he thought it would blow up, he would love it.

The director then started talking in a normal voice.

She was supposed to come home

I can picture my mother out in the field picking strawberries for supper. That would be it – just fresh biscuits and strawberries. She loved picking berries, and when they were ripe she would be out there for hours, kneeling down in the big fields around the house. You could look, and finally see her just visible above the grass. My father would go with her to pick raspberries and blackberries. He was in the woods a lot, hunting or cutting wood and he would often bring a bouquet of something for her. He was actually quite artistic and could arrange things nicely.

I don't remember my mother ever going to a doctor for anything. She hated them. She even had some of us kids at home with no doctor. She would say, "I am not going to a god damn doctor. If you go, they will always find something wrong."

She broke her leg a few years before she died and had not gone to see anyone. My father was dragging her in a chair or on a carpet, sliding it from the bedroom to the kitchen. I was the spokesman for us kids, so I was elected to tell her she had to go see a doctor. She agreed to go to Med-Now, over in Ellsworth.

So she got in and the doctor wanted to do lab work, tests, etc. You know how it works. She told him, "There is the goddamn leg. Fix the goddamn leg or go to hell." So what could they do? They just splinted it or something and sent her home. It was weeks before she could walk to any degree.

My sister Sandy was the steady one as my mother and father got to the point where they needed help. My mother checked out first. She was admitted to the hospital and died a few days later. I don't know why. She just died. She was supposed to come home the next day. Anyway, the night before she went in, I was elected to tell my father that my mother should go to a hospital. We just didn't feel he could care for her any longer. So I convinced my father that she should go the next morning. Boy, it's hard to tell your father something when he had always been the one in control.

I went into my mother's room. It was dark and smelled quite bad. Not very pleasant. She was sick. Anybody could tell that. She had been messing herself for a time but never went to doctors, as I have told you. I talked to her for a few minutes and said goodbye. I tried real hard to tell her I loved her, but just couldn't do it. I never saw her again.

When I got home that night, I had to call Sandy and tell her what had taken place. She knew what I wanted and said, "You want me to go over and clean her up and get her ready to go to the hospital, don't you?" What a lousy thing to ask your sister to do. Later, Sandy told me that my mother said, "Let me go for a couple of more weeks and you won't have to worry about me." She was angry about our plan to take her to a hospital and said, "I hate my family."

I have a hard time getting that part of my life out of my mind. As I have told you, of all the things I have done in my life, the things I regret most, yes let me repeat, the things I regret most, are the things *I did not do*, not the things I did.

After my mother died, Sandy was just as attentive with my father – paying his bills, doing things for him, and visiting him just about every day after working at a taxing job. Boy, you sure can't beat a person like that. I have always liked her a lot and would defend her to the death.

Never a dreamer

My mother and Pauline, your mother's mother, sort of grew up together and visited from time to time when we were young. I understand we actually played together when we were about age six. Anyway, up until the first day of high school I never saw her and knew practically nothing about her or her family.

My father had started working in Aurora and was going right by the house where Pauline and Irving lived, on Route 179 on the way out to Waltham. My mother had called Pauline and was going to spend the day with her and have my father pick her up when he came back from Aurora. I went along because it was the first day of school and I would be able to walk to high school with your mother. Back then we thought nothing of walking for miles. We never hitchhiked. Your mother used to walk to town every day when she worked at the restaurant in Ellsworth. It must have been seven miles but that was no big deal. A person can walk about four miles an hour, so in a couple of hours you could make it just fine.

We started out walking together to school. I remember quite well, I walked near the tar and she walked in the sand. She stayed away from me, really keeping her distance. I just had to walk in the road, because if I moved closer to her when a car came, she would move over more and end up in the ditch. That was the freshman year. I really raised hell during the freshman and sophomore (2nd) year and she was the last thing on my mind. I don't know where it all started really, but around the end of the sophomore year, we started going together. Nobody would believe it, because nobody ever saw us talking.

The summer after my sophomore year, I worked at a restaurant named *Luchini's* and we dated some. We went to Grange in Surry and rode in Harold Archer's car to the meetings. She was always good at Grange and went on to the state Grange with good standing. I remember one time we were going to a high school function and I had a 1941 Plymouth. It was not much, but it was a car. My mother decided to go, and several others. I was responsible to pick up and deliver. I never forgot it. My mother rode in the front seat with me and your

Robert and Velma Stevens on their wedding day, August, 1958. Attendants were Marilyn Saunders and Gary Leavitt.

mother sat in someone's lap in the back seat. It sure spoiled my night out!

After that, we called each other some. When I had a car, I would go to her house on Route 179 and pick her up, but I never had any money. I remember putting kerosene in a can, so I could put some in the car if I ran out on the way home. Those old cars would run on just about anything. We would go to the dances, in Surry mostly.

I never thought much about her family. I liked both her parents, and her brother Sonny and I got along very well. She was the oldest, as you know. Irving and Pauline seemed to get along ok and the house was always clean and it seemed to have some order to it. Even though I was young, I had some idea of what I wanted for a wife. I was always told to look at the future mother-in-law to see what your wife might look like after years of use. I did look at Pauline, and decided to get married anyway. She definitely did not like me. I was always upbeat and I think that bothered her. Something sure did. If I used the bathroom, she would wait outside the door and as I came out, she would brush by me and clean up after me, muttering all the time.

We moved in with them for about a year while I was building our house. During part of the year, I only worked until 4:00 and she would have supper cooked and over with before I got home. When I started working until 5:00, she would move it up that same day to be done and finished when I got home.

Irving and I got along quite well. He told your mother I did not know anything, but she married me anyway. We were class couple in our senior year and planned to get married as soon as we got out. After we graduated, I got an apartment on Hancock Street in Ellsworth for nine dollars a week and lived there until we got married. We lived there for a year, and then moved to an apartment on Bridge Hill.

After we were married, your mother began studying the Bible, but I didn't join her until a few years later. I was busy working, and thought it was a waste of time. I did not think too much about religion. I went to the Methodist church in Surry Village when I was young. I don't remember my father and mother going at all, except I was in a Christmas play once at the church, and I think they both attended. Mostly it was a "before Christmas and Easter Sunday" thing. I don't ever remember going on any regular basis. The Bonsey family ran a church in a little cabin next to them on the Neck. It was the Salvation Army. I thought the Salvation Army only rang a bell and collected money at Christmastime, but I guess not. I think they came up the Neck and picked us kids up. I am sure my father would not have done it. I only went there several times and I don't remember anything about what we might have been taught.

My beliefs were pretty basic. I did not believe in Hell. I really thought it was bad enough right here, without going for more grief. So I would argue that point with anyone. I sort of thought I was living my life good enough. I tried to treat people fairly, but anybody that treated me and mine badly, then I would plot as to how I was going to make their life miserable somehow. I really did spend time thinking how I could do that!

I worked a lot; more than anybody that I know now, or ever have known. There would actually be days I would not see you kids at all. Up in the morning and back after you went to bed. It was something I knew I could do, and in most cases, did well. It was very important to me not to ask help from anybody. I built our house all by myself - worked all day at a job and half of the night on the house. I had a lot of energy and could do it.

Your mother and I pretty much agreed on most things and seemed to be always able to work things out. She had the ability to get along with very little if we needed to. I remember one week, I wanted a gun for sale in Bangor for $11. We were usually only spending $10 a week for groceries. She thought about it, and figured she could get by with what we had for the week. I was making $57 a week at the time. I think when you were born in 1961, I was making $62 a week before taxes. If I was honest and leveled with her, she would make do.

I remember when all of you were still young. She called me at work and asked if we could go to a restaurant that night. I had about $30 and told her that was all I would have for some time. She hung up and talked it over with you kids, asking if you would be willing to get by for the week (probably eating beans or something else that didn't cost much.) Maybe you remember it. We went to *Sing's*, a Polynesian place in Bangor, and had a wonderful time. We actually did things like that a lot. We always tried to fit in fun things even though I had squat for money. I just knew how to work and mostly with my hands, so there never was a lot of money.

I don't think many people are born with a good ability to raise children, but we seriously tried to do the best we could. We both talk many, many times, about the things we should have done differently. She has the best memory of the two of us. She remembers what all of you kids like and dislike and she is the most generous one of us. I have had a good ride and a nice time and very few regrets. I mostly regret things I did not do, not the things I did. Time is running out, though. I can see it, and think more about it than I should. An old saying is, "If you live long enough, you will die of something." My three brothers are already gone. Guess who has to be next?

I have talked to a lot of older people and asked them if they have had a friend and they always say, "Oh, sure, I have lots of friends." But when I ask them how many in their life they could tell anything to, they will say, "Maybe only one in a lifetime, and maybe not even that." Your mother is the closest one I would call a friend.

I never thought I could have as good a life as my classmates had. When our relatives came for a family reunion, I really thought they were rich, or at least very well off, and I never, ever, had any thoughts of having a better life than what my mother and father had. I was always ashamed to talk to my parents about how much money I made or how well I was doing.

I was never a dreamer and have most always been satisfied with what I have. To me, the most tangible assets I have are family, and they have always been what I tried to hang on to. I always try to know where they are and how they are doing. It has been hard to do sometimes, getting them to keep in touch, but I try.

The old shed, shown here in 2014, is the only thing left on the property where the Stevens family lived.

The old shed

Recently, Amanda, my granddaughter, and her husband, Chris, went to Surry to see if anything was left of the old homestead. I was surprised that they found an old shed still on the property. I thought everything was removed after my brother sold all the land.

Our old shed was made of wood and covered on the sides with metal from old Humpty Dumpty potato chip cans. I believe that company is still in business. The cans were flattened and nailed onto the shingles, with the lettering facing the inside. The floor was made out of small trees about three inches wide and they would be laid together and then chain-sawed between them to make them fit better. Worked pretty good for an old wood shed. Anyway, my father was running that chain saw between them and it bucked back and hit him in the face. Took part of his nose off and hit his forehead, plus ruining his glasses. He was a mess, with blood everywhere. You can imagine how much blood there would be with a head wound. He drove himself to the hospital some 15 miles away. He didn't even go into the house to tell my mother. Said she would worry too much.

After finding out there was something left of the old homestead - the shed – it was burning in me to find out if it was the original one, so I went over to Surry and met the Bennetts who bought the remaining 30 acres from my brother. Mr. Bennett demolished the house and all the buildings, except the shed. He restored it enough to store some hand tools. Though it is in rough shape, he will use it for a while. The Bennetts are from Massachusetts and intend to move here permanently. It was a pleasure to meet them and one of their Greyhound dogs, Henry. They were more than glad to have me look the old shed over and just let my mind go back some.

Anyway, that shed was a blast from the past. You can see from the picture Amanda took.

Conclusion

In 2012, at the age of 72, my father, Robert Stevens, retired as plant supervisor for Union River Telephone Company in Aurora, Maine, where he lived and worked for 32 years. Many in that rural community know him and love him.

He and my mother, Velma, now reside in the coastal town of Bucksport. They were "class couple" when they graduated from Ellsworth High School in 1958 and are still happily married. They raised five children: John, me, Kevin, Maryellen, and Paul. They provided us with a solid foundation in life and instilled in each of us a strong work ethic, a desire to help others, and a love for one another.

Catherine A. Serrao

Robert and Velma in St. Augustine, Florida in 2012

A brief family history – in case you want to know more

Russell K. Stevens was born in Surry, Maine, on June 14, 1909, to Omar J. Stevens and Amanda Henry. Omar and Amanda had eight children: Maurice (Big Red), Russell, Irving, Harold (Little Red), Omar, Sidney Bettina (Betty), and Dorothy. The family bounced around from Surry to Massachusetts in his early years, traveling to where his father, Omar, could get work. They were living in Ballardvale, Massachusetts, when Russell and Omar came down with scarlet fever and pneumonia. The entire house was quarantined and only his aunt came to bring them food. Russell got better, but his father died. Omar was buried in Andover, Massachusetts at the age of 42, leaving Amanda with seven children to care for. Big Red, 16 at the time, began working in a metal foundry to help support the family.

At the age of 14, Russell was sent to Surry to live with his grandmother, Sabrina Kane Stevens (wife of Marshall Stevens), and her daughter, Clara Cary, and husband, Jim. He attended Surry schools for a time but only made it to 4th grade. By the age of 17, with jobs scarce, he went off to California to pick fruit along with the Mexicans. After that, he worked at a cow ranch in Hueneme, and then hitchhiked to Portland, Oregon, where he signed on to a salmon fishing vessel heading to Alaska. During the next few years, he worked on a steamer loaded with grain going to Ireland, and even spent a little time in a jail in Cardiff, Wales. He traveled by ship to the Cape Verde Islands, through the Panama Canal to New Zealand, then to Australia, and back again to the United States. He jumped ship in Texas and never went back to sea.

By 1927 his mother, Amanda, had moved to Ashville, Ohio, with the Kibbee family. Russell's sister Dorothy remembered leaving Massachusetts in the middle of the night. It seems Amanda was pregnant by Ken Kibbee (her daughter Ruth came from that relationship), but Ken's wife was pregnant at the same time. The two women ended up giving birth nearly the same time. For a while Amanda lived in a converted box car in the Kibbee's back yard. Needless to say, it was a very interesting arrangement. Several of Amanda's children were still with her but the others had been scattered about – Betty got left behind with a couple in Massachusetts who had been their neighbors, one of the boys was in Surry with his grandmother, Russell was out to sea, Irving was riding the rails, and Big Red was still working at the foundry.

By the time Ruth was two years old, Amanda was contacted by her sister-in-law, Clara Cary, who offered her the old Thatcher place, nestled on blueberry grounds, if she would return to Surry and take care of Sabrina. Amanda quickly accepted, but the move back to Maine was not without problems. She had very little money for the trip. Son Harold bought an old Dodge car, and they left Ashville in 1929. Russell had returned from sea to be with them on their journey back to Surry to join the rest of his family. In addition to mechanical problems, they had numerous flat tires along the way. The rubber on those old tires was not like it is today and it was not uncommon to have several flat tires in a week's time. They carried a patching kit and all the tools necessary to do what they had to do – jack up the car, break down the tire, take out the tube, and put on another patch. In those days, folks would patch up a tire many times before it would be replaced.

Amanda and her gang made it as far as New York when the car broke down for good. The whole family was put up by a church mission of some sort and after a few days they were put on a train that brought them into the Ellsworth station. From there to Surry, they rode the stage. It was the spring of 1929, and the Great Depression was setting in, so the boys left Surry frequently to get work, returning as often as they could. Amanda took up housekeeping, caring for Sabrina (Biney) until her death in 1931.

At about this time, Freeman (Father) Burns came into the picture. He was 26 years old and Amanda was 45 at the time of their marriage in 1931. Russell and Little Red often spoke of him, but never in a positive manner. Freeman was a bum, someone who couldn't even support himself. Amanda had a lot of problems after the death of Omar and inevitably made some mistakes, and Freeman Burns was one of them.

She had not been with Burns too long before Russell and his brothers were home for a visit. They could see that she was being treated badly. One night the boys got drinking hard and after Freeman went to bed, just the next room away, they started discussing what they were going to do to him when he came out. He must have heard the plotting because he went out the window and was never heard from again!

After the departure of Freeman Burns, Amanda continued living in the Thatcher place, raising Ruth and providing a home base for the older children. All of them stayed there at one time or another during the 1930's and contributed what they could. It was during these years that Daniel J. (DJ) Sexton came onto the scene. Evidently he and Amanda lived together for a couple of years until his drinking led to a break-up and he moved out on his own.

Sometime in the early '30's Red and Russell went with Captain Gilbert from Rockland, taking the ship *Lavolta* out of Surry Bay. This ship was being towed to Salem, Massachusetts, to be made into a sister ship looking like the Mayflower. The *Lavolta*, renamed *Arrabella*, was a ship owned by *Whitcomb and Haines* of Ellsworth, Maine, and had been moored in Surry Bay for a few years. (The *Nellie Grant*, a ship that was moored with her, was lost at sea with all hands off the Portland coast in 1925. The *Nellie* was captained by Russell's uncle, Captain Newel Cane, or Kane, as it was spelled at the time.) After arriving in Salem and helping with the *Arrabella*, Russell stayed around the Boston area for a while. He hung around a few gyms and boxed or wrestled, living in a boiler house in Quincy. It had a few bunks and he shared it with a couple of seamen. He also spent some weekends with Big Red and his wife, Hon. Big Red was miserable, but Russell got along well with Hon and they enjoyed playing cards together.

Russell came home to Maine to cut wood, and in the spring of 1939, at age 29, he married Dorathy Mae Mack, just 18 years old. Robert was born the following year on February 14.

While in Ellsworth one night, Russell got drunk and his car slid into a truck sander. He was arrested by Winnie Garland, an Ellsworth cop, and ended up in jail. Apparently he woke up the next morning, and remembered nothing from the night before. He spent a week there, got probation, and lost his license.

Figuring he could get along better in Massachusetts, he hitchhiked there and stayed with his old friends, Jack and Gladys Nobles. He was like a son to them. Gladys must have been a poor housekeeper, because Russell said they always had bedbugs, and their son Jack constantly had his hand in his pants scratching at crabs. Within a couple of weeks Russell found a job in a broom factory and he sent for Dorathy and Robert. They spent the next couple of years living in Willimantic, Massachusetts.

By 1944 the family returned to Surry for good, just in time for Robert to start school. It was early in the year, and the ice was still in because Russell had a record of his smelt fishing that spring. They moved into a one-room camp built by his brother, Irving. Another room was added after all of the kids were born, but it was never more than 144 square feet. The house sat on a hill with a view of Union River Bay and the distant hills of Acadia National Park. By 1947 four more children were born to Russell and Dorathy: Thomas, Wesley, Walter, and Sandra.

Made in the USA
Middletown, DE
21 May 2022

66041373R00096